The Leaving of Loughrea

An Irish Family in the Great Famine

STEPHEN LALLY

authorHOUSE®

AuthorHouse™
1663 Liberty Drive
Bloomington, IN 47403
www.authorhouse.com
Phone: 1-800-839-8640

© 2013 by Stephen Lally. All rights reserved.

No part of this book may be reproduced, stored in a retrieval system, or transmitted by any means without the written permission of the author.

Published by AuthorHouse   05/01/2013

ISBN: 978-1-4817-8824-3 (sc)
ISBN: 978-1-4817-8826-7 (hc)
ISBN: 978-1-4817-8825-0 (e)

Front cover illustration
'Emigrant Ship in Dublin Bay Sunset' by Edwin Hayes.
By permission of the National Gallery of Ireland.

This book is printed on acid-free paper.

Because of the dynamic nature of the Internet, any web addresses or links contained in this book may have changed since publication and may no longer be valid. The views expressed in this work are solely those of the author and do not necessarily reflect the views of the publisher, and the publisher hereby disclaims any responsibility for them.

To my grandchildren

This story is written to tell you who you are and where you have come from. It touches on historical facts and situations to illustrate the lives of our Lally family and how your flesh and blood lived 200 years ago in Ireland. It shows the unbelievable contrast between your ancestors' lives and the life you lead today.

This book is also dedicated to the grandchildren of all the Irish who left for new lands during the Great Famine.

Contents

1. Introduction—Leave No Stone Unturned 1
2. The Lallys of Knockatogher 13
3. Patrick Lally's Life in Ireland 26
4. The Real Hard Facts of Irish Life 47
5. The Underlying Reasons for Irish Problems 62
6. Attempts at Solutions to Irish Problems 78
7. The Great Famine 87
8. Leaving for England—Patrick Lally 115
9. Leaving for North America—Patrick and Mary Lally 124
10. Leaving for Australia—Mary Anne, Margaret and Mary Lally 139
11. A New World, 1848 168
12. Bibliography 175
13. Acknowledgements 177

1. Introduction—Leave No Stone Unturned

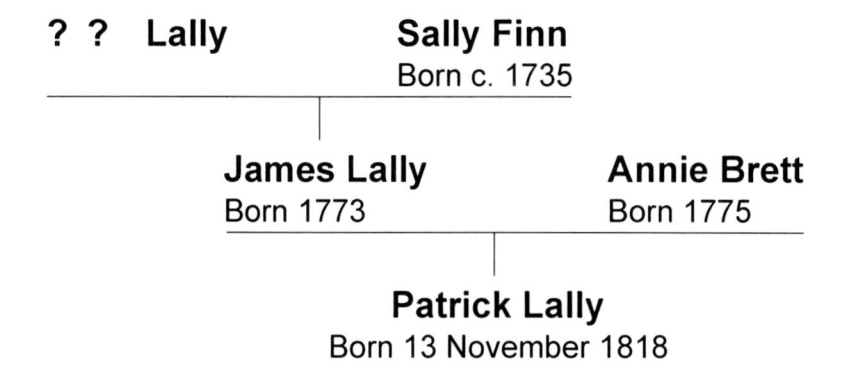

? ? Lally **Sally Finn**
　　　　　　　Born c. 1735

　　　　James Lally　　**Annie Brett**
　　　　Born 1773　　　　Born 1775

　　　　　　Patrick Lally
　　　　　Born 13 November 1818

This story is incredible. It will be beyond your wildest imaginings, and the description of the lives and deaths people endured in Ireland in the early 1800s will fill you with horror. But you must read on because this story is about you. If you are a Lally or have a Lally family in your past, then this is about your ancestors, but this is a story for anybody with Irish blood and who has ancestors who left Ireland in the 1840s. By rare chance enough information has survived to enable us to briefly glimpse how this particular family lived in 1821. Then our story broadens out to describe life in general in the west of Ireland at that time and how conditions must have shaped our ancestors not only in terms of what they did but also how they, and others, thought at that time and why such terrible things were inflicted on them and the whole Irish nation.

In case it's necessary, I should make clear right at the beginning of this story that Ireland was under British rule for 750 years until the 1920s. In 1801 Ireland became a part of the United Kingdom as much as were England, Wales, and Scotland. Ireland was ruled from London, and this was the nub of the situation. It was the heart of the reasons for Ireland's problems that so affected our ancestors during the years this book studies, 1818 to 1848.

The ancestor I know most about is Patrick Lally, whose parents were James and Annie Lally. Patrick, to you, my grandchildren, was your great, great, great, great-grandfather. For James and Annie you can add another 'great'. They must have had brothers and sisters, aunts, uncles, and cousins but records about them no longer exist. In England, and from about 1860 in Ireland, it is possible to put together families by cross referencing information from censuses and birth, marriage, and death records. It is more difficult in the earlier period we are looking at here, and in Ireland it is virtually impossible. I've looked everywhere.

During the Great Famine some of the highest death rates were among priests, as they tended the sick, so, as we see later, many just couldn't cope with keeping records as well. Looking at the surviving originals in tiny scrawl, in faded ink, with different priests entering different information in different order, in semi-Latin, in small, plain, paper notebooks, it's not surprising that so much has been lost. Even the Irish censuses have been destroyed, and only tiny fragments remain. I concentrated my searches on nine parishes, Loughrea and the eight parishes immediately adjoining it*, but, from what few records survive, I found nothing—at first.

* The nine parishes were:
1. Loughrea, 2. Bullaun, Grange and New Inn, 3. Cappataggle and Kilreekil, 4. Carrabane, Kilconickney, Kilconieran and Lickerigg,
5. Craughwell, 6. Kilchreest and Issertkelly, 7. Killeenadeema and Aille, 8. Kiltullagh and Killimordally, 9. Leitrim, Kilcooley and Kilmeen.

The entry in the records of Nazareth House showing Patrick's admission and departure details and the names of his parents. This set me on my search in Ireland. Here he calls himself James.

Before we start looking back at his life, we'd better summarise what we actually know about Patrick Lally before 1848—when we know he was in London. Patrick was better remembered by my contemporary family members than even more recent members of the Lally family, so he must have been quite some character. Also, my long searches through records in London, turning over page after page, have occasionally brought up priceless pieces of information.

Firstly, it has come down five generations and through several branches of the family that Patrick came to England from Loughrea, in County Galway, in the province of Connaught, in the west of Ireland. He must have looked on the Loughrea area as home, and his children passed this fact on to their grandchildren. My Aunt Vera told it to me when I asked in the 1960s. Patrick also confirmed this in 1887 when he was admitted to the Nazareth House Roman Catholic Home for the Aged Poor in Hammersmith, West London, and this record survives today. Also written there are the names of his father and mother: James Lally and Annie Brett. This record also gives his exact date of birth; 13 November 1818. That he was a Catholic is also confirmed by his marriage in the Catholic

Chapel at Isleworth, west of London, on 27 July 1851, when he was thirty-three years old, and by the baptisms of his children.

Being a Catholic set his place in Irish society. He signed his own name in the wedding register, which suggests a probability that he could read and write, so perhaps he was not right at the bottom of that society. On the marriage certificate he gave his father's occupation as publican. He stated at his wedding that he was a bachelor so, unless he lied to the priest, he didn't marry while in Ireland. Bearing in mind that he left Ireland when in his late twenties, this was unusual.

He was, as is said of all the Irish, very fond of children and would sing to them and his grandchildren and tell them stories. He played the Irish fiddle well. His trade from the first record of him in England, the 1851 census, to his death in 1895 was consistently 'Gardener'. Both fiddle playing and gardening suggest a delicacy of the fingers, although 'delicacy' may be too fine a word to describe the man himself. In the 1851 census he was shown as 'gardener and in charge of the house' of Lord Ernest Bruce, which was a responsible and trusted job with an English Lord and may tell us Patrick had good references or a manner that inspired trust.

In later life, when he flew into a rage or had drunk too much he would shout in a language nobody could understand, which I would suggest was Gaelic. He said his name was James in the 1851 census but Patrick in 1861. At his wedding and at the baptisms of all but one of his children he was named as Patrick. Later in life he generally called himself James. I would take this to mean he was baptised Patrick but later took his father's name of James. We shall call him Patrick.

I set out on the almost impossible task of looking at Patrick's earlier life back home in Ireland. Many stories of him after he came to London have survived in the family for 150 years but little about Ireland. Perhaps he never spoke about his life in Ireland. Perhaps it was all too dreadful for him to recall. Perhaps he had something to hide. Perhaps . . .

Having thought I had completed this story and while browsing one of the plethora of websites related to Irish family history I noticed a new service on 'Ireland Reaching Out' by which it is possible to contact local volunteers. So remote was the chance of finding anything that I said to possible contacts on the website that I was writing only on the principle of leaving no stone unturned. Back came the information from a fragment of the 1821 census, which all the official sources had overlooked, about our Lally family in the townland of Knockatogher in the parish of Kiltullagh just six miles north of Loughrea. (The name is pronounced 'Knockato'er', the 'gh' being silent.)

The rare fragment from the 1821 census.

How often can one be 100 per cent certain of a part of a family tree? In England it is relatively easy because of the extent of surviving records, but not in Ireland. However, here, in this thousand-to-one chance, was a Lally family with the right names and a Patrick of the right age and within my search area. Also, bearing in mind the great rarity in Ireland of Patrick's mother's maiden Brett, there were Brett families living nearby. To give me that 100 per cent certainty I'd need to check if there wasn't, by coincidence, a similarly matching family elsewhere in my nine parishes but this information doesn't survive. So it's reasonable to give a certainty of 95 per cent that this is our Lally family and on that basis I have completed this story. This 1821 snapshot of our Lally family when Patrick was a toddler gives him a place in Irish society from which we can better describe his young life in the years that followed, and we can create an image of this interesting man.

To find one such snapshot is a freak of good fortune. Not even the luck of the Irish could permit another. Lally was a good old Connaught name and rare elsewhere in Ireland, but thorough searches of surviving records and newspapers turn up nothing certain. There are several James, Patrick, and Mary Lallys but you cannot cross reference these names to be able to say they were our family. In Pigot's occupational directory and Slater's commercial directories of 1824 and 1846 no Lallys are shown as owning shops, bars, or other businesses in the area. Griffith's valuation of all property in 1856 shows six plots rented by a Lally in Loughrea, five by John Lally who may have been the same man.

If the search for James, Annie, and Patrick is widened to newspapers and other records we find a few as witnesses in court—to a murder and an unlawful assembly, for example. In July 1839 a Patrick Lally is accused of rape but at Galway Assizes is sentenced to a year in prison on the lesser charge of common assault. Was he our ancestor? In September 1844 a

Patrick Lally was sentenced to transportation for fifteen years for shooting and wounding a man in Cooldara while stealing wheat. 'Because he was starving', he said. This wasn't our Patrick because Australian records survive showing that he was pardoned ten years later for good behaviour and by this time we know our Patrick was in London.

In January 1847 Anne Lally was assaulted in Loughrea Workhouse but was she 'our' Annie Lally? In December 1848 Mrs Lally and her family were granted assisted emigration by the Loughrea Board of Guardians so they could go with her husband who had been sentenced to transportation. Several times in the early 1840s nine-year-old Mary Lally was jailed with hard labour for begging.

On 17 January 1837 an Anne Lally died in Cappataggle, seven miles north east of Loughrea. Patrick's mother, Anne, would have then been sixty two, and Cappataggle is within my area of search. It is very tempting to say, 'Surely this must be Patrick's mother', but there is no back-up information with this death record—no named relations or age. Of all the leads, this is the one, at Cappataggle, that is the most interesting. It may indicate where the family moved to after Knockatogher, but there is no proof.

They sound a rough lot, these Lallys, but life was very rough in those times, and it must be remembered that it is criminals and the higher classes who are mentioned most often in the press. I'd like to think that not all our family were criminals, and they certainly were not in the higher classes at this time.

To what extent were all these Lallys related? In the area around Loughrea there were not many Lally families. Based on the number in Griffith's valuation of 1856 and the overall decline in population prior to that, one can say that by the beginning of the 1840s there were up to eight Lally families in the town of Loughrea itself. In the eight parishes immediately surrounding the town, in the catchment area of eight miles round about Loughrea, there were probably up to another twenty families; let's say twenty to thirty in all. In a futile attempt to link these Lally families I have been in contact with other people who, like me, have today gone back looking for their Lally ancestors who lived in the Loughrea area at the same time. I have not been able to discover any positive family links but have included in this book three of these Lally groups, in addition to our own family, because they lived in the Loughrea area at the same time, they lived through the dramatic events I will describe, and all were forced to leave their beloved homeland. These family groups are:—

Patrick and Bridget Lally Born 1790 and 1795	Martin and Eliza Lally	Patrick and Marion Lally
Their son **Patrick Lally** b.1817 and his wife **Mary Byrne**	Their daughters **Mary Ann Lally** b.1833 **Margaret Lally** b.1835	Their daughter **Mary Lally** b.1833
Left for Philadelphia, USA in 1843	These 3 girls left together for Sydney, Australia as orphans in 1848	
Patrick & Bridget also had a son, Matthew, b.1816, and perhaps another son, John.	Their son John Lally, b.1839, left for Sydney, Australia in 1859	

Patrick and Mary Lally left for America from Loughrea, and sisters Mary Ann and Margaret Lally were sent to Australia from Loughrea Workhouse. Mary Lally left on the same ship to Australia but from the parish of Ballymacward, just to the north of Knockatogher where our own Lally family had lived. She was the right age to have been the Mary Lally imprisoned

8

for begging but there's no proof. There's a chance we are all related and that they met in church, school, or in Loughrea on market days. We'll never know for sure, but I've assumed there's a link and have called them cousins so I can include their stories. This has allowed me to look more completely at life in Ireland at this time and from three specific points of view, particularly when describing that most common feature of Irish life—emigration.

Even before the Great Famine of the mid 1840s hunger was commonplace and starvation not unusual. What a dreadful common inheritance that was. It was this Great Famine, as opposed to minor ones, that triggered the mass emigration of the Irish people, many Lallys among them, who had no option but to leave Loughrea. This is the melting pot from which our family arose and spread all over the world. They led lives that you will find difficult to imagine but which I have attempted to describe here. Read on. The story starts in truly dramatic fashion.

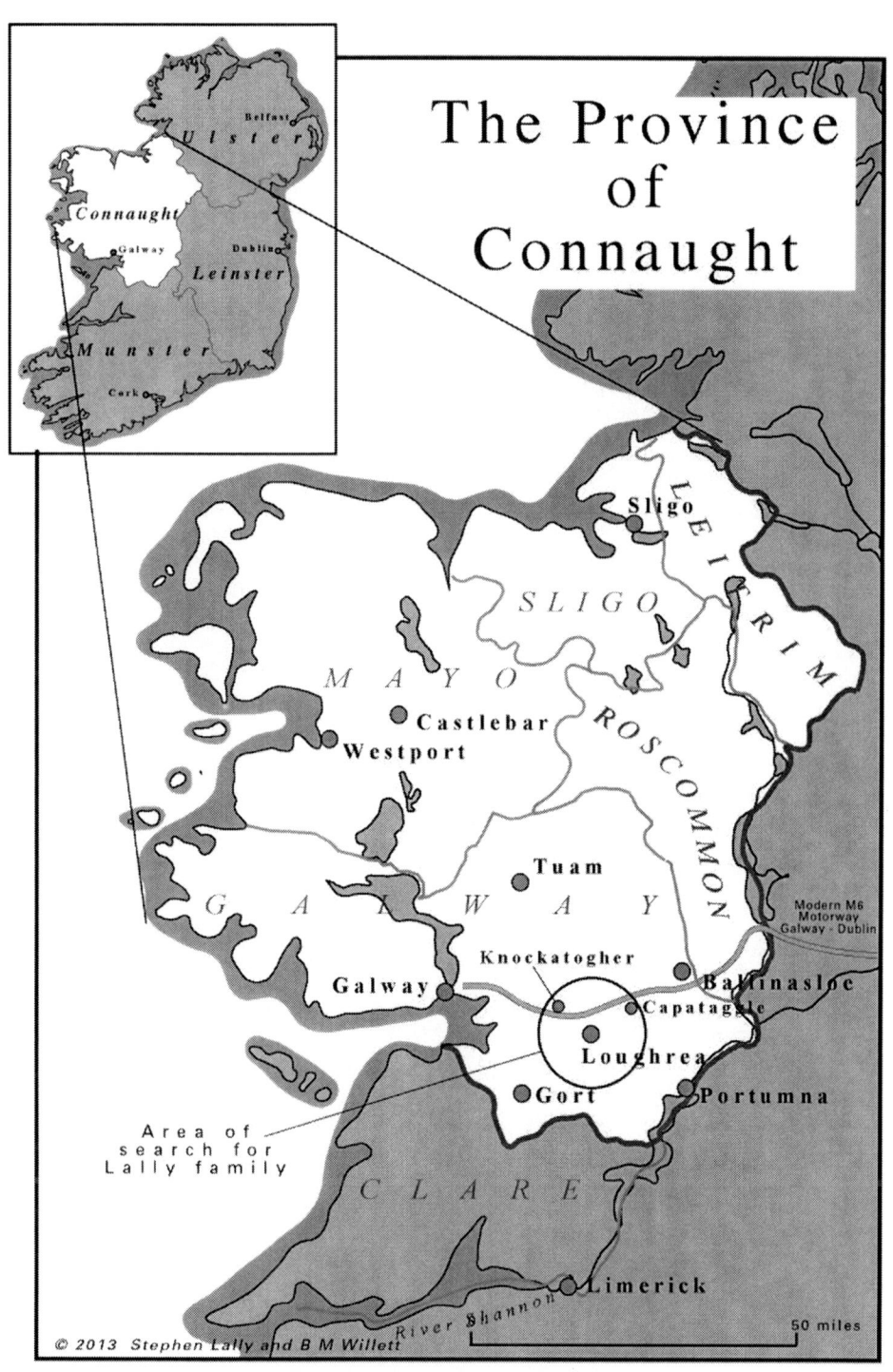

A map of the Province of Connaught.

The Freeman's Journal,
AND DAILY COMMERCIAL ADVERTISER.

PRICE—FIVE-PENCE.   DUBLIN, THURSDAY, JULY 19, 1821.   VOL. LV.

CORONER'S INQUEST.

The following has been transmitted to us by a Correspondent at Loughrea:—

On Tuesday, the 10.h inst. a young man, about 22 years of age, named William Lally, who lived with his parents at Knockatoher, near Dunsandle, in this county, was, about the hour of eleven o'clock in the forenoon, sitting in his father's house, in company with his grandmother, Sally Lally, alias Finn, Sally Lally, his sister, and four younger children, (also his brothers and sisters) when, in a violent paroxysm of rage, without any apparent provocation, began to beat violently his sister Sally, a girl about 18 years of age, expressing at the same time his determined resolution of putting an end to her life. The poor girl, in terror, made the best resistance she was capable of, and fortunately escaped from his hands, first into an adjoining room, and whilst he was seeking for a weapon to put his threats into execution, succeeded in making her way out of the house, together with her four children. In the mean time the monster having seized an iron spade, was rushing with the intent of preventing the escape of his sister, when the grandmother interposed, hoping to disarm his rage, and prevent its consequences; upon which he struck with said weapon the latter to the ground, by a mortal blow on the head! This not satisfying the monster, he proceeded to sever the head from the body, which he effected with all the circumstances of horrible brutality, by repeated blows; and in consequence of the bluntness of the weapon, he so mangled the entire head and neck as to leave not a trace of either behind, except the disconnected parts that remained scattered over the floor, walls, doors and windows! Thus having secured himself from the interference or opposition of the grandmother, the murderer, in his thirst for blood, rushed in pursuit of his sister; on his way he observed an old woman, named Eleanor Coan, alias Nicholson, and a young girl, named Bridget Cannon, (both of the neighbourhood) flying in terror into a neighbouring house, the door of which they bolted. He pursued them with his murderous weapon, but finding the door closed and fastened, began with violent strokes to break it open; while he was threatening to enter by violence, one of the children within unbolted the door, and retired with the young girl (Bridget Cannon) for security into the next room. The old woman, Eleanor Coan, being the first person he met as he entered, he gave her, with said weapon, a mortal blow on the head, and immediately put a period to her existence!—While he continued his work of blood in treating the latter victim nearly in the same manner as he did the former, the young girl (Bridget Cannon) with three children, in terror of their lives, fortunately unnoticed by the murderer, made their escape. The alarm was immediately given to his father, who was at husbandry about four acres off; upon his approaching, the murderer made a blow at him with the spade, but fortunately without effect—informing him at the same time he had killed his mother, and would also kill him and others. The father having at length procured assistance, succeeded in securing and binding him.

Mr. Cloran, Coroner having received information of this melancholy catastrophe, immediately called out a party of the Police to accompany him to the tragic scene, distant from his residence at Loughrea, about six miles. On his arrival, and seeing the unfortunate victim, he desired to see the murderer, who was shewn to him, bound with ropes, and whom he immediately gave in charge to the Police, until the issue of the Inquisition, on which he immediately proceeded. It appeared from the detail of evidences, that the unfortunate perpetrator of these atrocious murders had been previously observed at intervals, to labour under mental derangement. The Jury found him "Guilty of Murder," in both cases; upon which, said Coroner committed him on that day to Loughrea prison, and was from thence transmitted on the 13th inst. to the county Gaol, Galway, to abide his trial at the next general Assizes.—*Connaught Journal.*

2. The Lallys of Knockatogher

Everybody yearns for something dramatic in their family story, a spectacular event that makes them famous and gets them in the national papers. But the violent murders described in such gruesome detail on the previous page brought infamy on the murderer and his family: our Lally family. James Lally, when he had run across his fields on that Tuesday morning in July 1821 and come upon this scene, may have chosen any of the horrors of Irish life; poverty, starvation, religious persecution or eviction, to what he was actually confronted with. His son William was known to be insane; it was his stated occupation in the 1821 census suggesting he was fit for nothing else. Yet now James' mother, was dead, along with a neighbour, and nothing could save his son from the rope following his brief trial and the verdict of 'Guilty of Murder'.

An idiot and his mother in Ireland

Four years later, in 1825, a survey was carried out to list those with five acres or more who had to pay tithes for the upkeep of the established Church of Ireland. The Lally family was not shown in Knockatogher so must have moved away. This perhaps was a sign of the stigma that fell on the family or just the shame of what had happened and the need to make a fresh start. By remote chance this fragment of the 1821 census has survived and can clearly be linked to the newspaper report. It gives us an opportunity to study a snapshot of our family which sets their position in society, after which they disappear again from records like nearly every other family. I believe they stayed in the vicinity of Loughrea because that was our Patrick's stated home town and, hopefully, Patrick was too young to remember anything of that fateful day.

So, putting the horror aside if we can, let's look at our family in 1821 of which we can learn a great deal from the April census and the July newspaper report.

Firstly we can see our family, three generations, living together. It would have been quite normal for the old grandmother, presumably widowed, to be living there. A family with ten or twelve children was to be expected, and the gaps in the children's ages suggest that most of them had moved away. Pat, our Patrick, one of the children shepherded away by Sally, was probably the youngest, even younger than his nephew, Charly.

A typical Connaught man.

It is perhaps odd that no six or eight-year-old children appear in the census. The whole family mucked in together, looking after each other while parents were busy or had had to move away to scrape a living. Annie is not mentioned in the description of the outrage. She may have been away at market or working nearby, which was just as well.

14

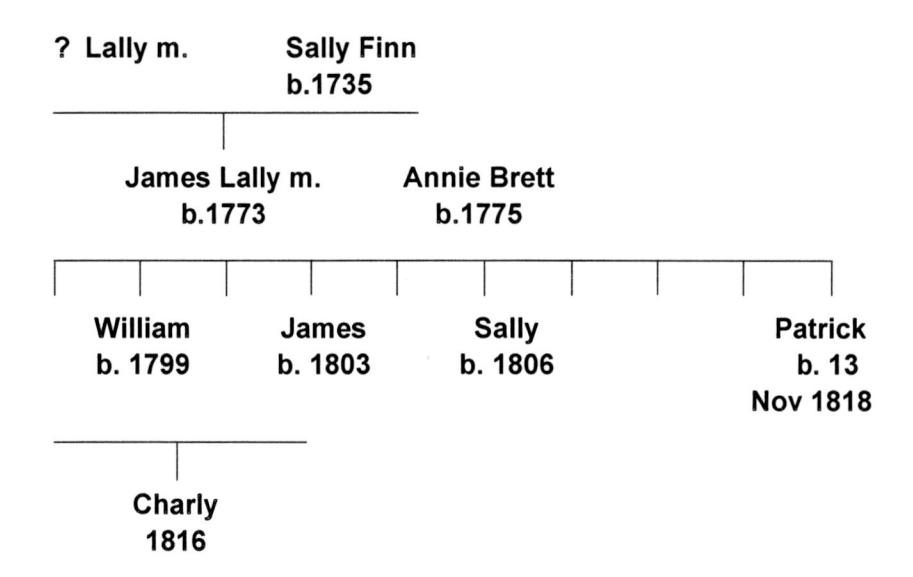

```
? Lally m.          Sally Finn
                    b.1735
───────────┬──────────────
    James Lally m.    Annie Brett
       b.1773            b.1775
  ┌────┬────┬────┬────┬────┬────┬────┬────┐
William   James      Sally            Patrick
b. 1799   b. 1803    b. 1806          b. 13
                                      Nov 1818
────┬────
  Charly
   1816
```

We are told in the newspaper report that the Lally house had floor, walls, doors, windows, and at least two rooms. The neighbouring house had doors that bolted and that were strong enough and fixed well enough to the walls to withstand an onslaught with a spade. James' and Annie's house would have been of mud or mud bricks and probably built by James himself. These details put the houses above average in size and quality. The Lally house had enough space for the seven people to sit on that Tuesday morning with Sally spinning her flax and the grandmother helping or looking after the children. An image of the type of house can be seen in the illustration, which gives no illusions as to the dilapidation, leaking roof, and damp mud floor.

A house like James Lally's.

Let's dispel any idea of modern conveniences at this early stage of our story. Water would have come from the river or pond. Waste would have been spread and then dug into the fields and the family's possessions may have extended to a couple of stools, an iron pot for cooking, and, if they were lucky, one bed. They would have had no use for a wardrobe or any other storage as there would have been nothing to store. As we shall see later, half the houses in Connaught were windowless mud cabins of one room, without even a chimney, so our family were relatively well off.

Knockatogher was, and still is, part of the parish of Kiltullagh-Killimordally, about six miles north of Loughrea and six miles east of Athenry. It was not a village in itself, but a collection of houses spread over 680 acres, just over a square mile. The border of this townland was only a line on a map but it is useful to help us imagine the view from the window and look of the land James Lally rushed across on that fateful morning.

The name Knockatogher means 'hill in the trackway through the bog' and, as its name implies, it is a dome of slightly raised land with few trees and was marked in places on the 1841 map as liable to flooding. Other than the Dooyertha River that ran along its southern boundary it had few features. The higher land was good agricultural land, and the small fields were divided by rough stone walls which, as the local stones were round, seemed unstable and held together more by ivy and trees than firm interlocking. The walls were three feet to four feet high (one metre) and also ran on either side of the sunken tracks, known as 'boreens', that crisscrossed the area linking the 'clachans' or small groups of houses.

Knockatogher had a centre, known to locals as 'the village', but only the locals would have recognised it as such. A local man, being typically less than five feet tall (one and a half metres), walking along a sunken boreen would not usually have been able to see over the wall, giving him a feeling of being closed in. While the overall terrain was flat, every field was undulating and roughly dug and planted irregularly by hand so the undulations and the walls and trees hid most distant views, enhancing this feeling of isolation.

The small, tumbledown, single-story houses were huddled together with stores of wood and peat and other useful things around them, almost giving the impression of being in the land, not on it. This was the overriding impression a visitor would have had: of isolation, being inward looking, almost claustrophobic, of nothing going on.

Running parallel to and north of the river was a main road from Galway and Athenry in the west to Ballinasloe and ultimately to Dublin in the east. In ancient times this had been the great highway from east to west: the Escir Riada or Sli Mor. The 1841 Ordnance Survey map shows houses scattered all along this road so travellers would have created what little activity there was in this quiet area

Add total silence to this slow, rural environment; there was no radio, no traffic, no drum of a distant motorway or plane overhead. The only sounds were perhaps children playing, birds singing, or a pig snuffling. How else could James Lally have heard the commotion surrounding the murders and the call for him to come from four acres away? There was neither clock nor watch to tell time, just the movement of the sun from dawn till dusk and after that, pitch black. No glow from distant street lights, just the light of the moon and stars. The myriad stars shining brightly in the unlit night sky would have convinced our family and their neighbours that they were a small part of a great plan, not, as today, the twenty-first century masters of the world.

Anyone standing on a raised piece of land and looking out at the view beyond this little world would have seen the sun glinting off the bogs in the near distance and spiky, tall, bog grasses and reeds. Through the mist would have been hills rising all around several miles away. You may have caught a glint of the sun off the Dooyertha River on the southern boundary of Knockatogher. This was a fast-flowing river, about two feet deep (sixty centimetres) at normal times and about thirty-three feet (ten metres) wide but often spreading out across marshy borders or splitting in two in places. A mile to the south east and near a river bridge was Rafford House. This was a four-storey square block with stabling and gardens, typical of many such houses. A bit further away was a corn mill on the river. To the south west the main road ran through the village of Kiltullagh, which was a collection of similar houses to those in Knockatogher but a recognizable village because it had a chapel, a corn mill near a bridge, a small single-storey, thatched beer house, and Kiltullagh House, another four-story, square mansion. A mile to the northeast of Knockatogher was Killimor Castle, again with outbuildings, gardens, and sheltered by trees.

The census of 1821 shows James Lally as a 'Farmer / Labourer' with six acres: an area perhaps 200 x 145 yards or 200 x 120 metres, which he would have dug and cared for entirely by hand. It was accepted that five productive acres were the minimum needed to support a family, and only landholders with five or more acres paid the hated tithes. So James just scraped by, as did his neighbours. He may have had a Connaught Pig, a common breed in this area because it ate virtually anything and therefore cost nothing to keep. The 1825 'Tithe Applotment Book' shows forty-nine landholders in Knockatogher and how many acres each farmed so we can tell that a typical plot here was three to seven acres and all James' neighbours were just scraping by with nothing to spare. In the 1821 census nearly 90 per cent of the men in Knockatogher were farmers or labourers, like James. The others were servants, and there was one wheelmaker, a tailor, a blacksmith, two shoemakers, and three linen weavers. On his land James would have had to grow potatoes to give the family their basic food. He probably grew flax because his wife and daughter were both flax spinners, as were more than 80 per cent of the other women who listed an occupation in the census. The presence of two corn mills nearby on the river suggests corn was grown locally. One can only guess whether other farm crops were grown there too.

Flax spinning would have augmented the family income, and Irish soil was ideal for growing flax plants, which needed wet, deep loam or peat. Flax had been introduced to the area in the 1600s by the D'Arcy family, owners of the big house in Kiltullagh. The plants were harvested by hand by pulling up the whole plant to maximise the length of the stems and fibres. Then the stems were 'retted', in rivers or ponds so that the woody parts of the stem rotted and the fibre could easily be separated. The best quality fibre was derived from field retting whereby the stems were laid in damp fields where the action of the dew separated the fibres. Then the fibres were taken from the stems by 'breaking' to remove the wood, 'scutching' to clean the fibres, and 'heckling' through a series of combs to finally produce individual threads. After drying, the spinners who normally worked in twos or threes, as did Anne and Sally, used one treadle spinning wheel to create the thread and a 'clock wheel' to stretch it and count it out. One hundred and twenty revolutions of the wheel wound three-hundred yards of yarn, called a 'cutt'. Twelve cutts made a 'hank', and four hanks were a 'spangle'. This whole process, from planting to spinning, would have been handled by the Lally family and by their neighbours. The final product went to market at the Loughrea Linen Hall—the best quality to become damask, lesser quality became linen, and the poorest quality to be rope.

What an idyllic scene of country folk working happily! Regrettably our story has few idyllic scenes. Flax spinning was hard, dirty work, poorly paid, and by the 1820s prices were falling nearly every year putting the cottage industry into sharp decline. Nobody would invest in modern manufacturing methods in Ireland, and by 1821 Hely Dutton, in his report on the state of Ireland, described the Loughrea Linen Hall as busy but in a 'wretched state of neglect and decay'. Weaving of linen had virtually disappeared by 1840, leaving the local people more dependent on a hand-to-mouth existence on potatoes.

Most travel was, of course, on foot. The spun flax may have been taken into Loughrea by cart, but in the early days of which we are talking, this would at best have been a cart with solid wooden wheels, which were cheaper than spoked wheels and easier to repair. Out in the country in the 1820s the wheel-less 'slide car' would still have been common. This was a sort of sleigh pulled by a donkey over the smooth and slippery wet ground.

Let's now turn our attention to the young children in our family in 1821, particularly to Pat who, little as he could imagine then, is to be the centre of our interest 200 years later. In 1818 he had been born into a world where the concept of childhood didn't exist and where, as soon as he was able, he had to take on adult responsibilities. Not for him the toys, books, and clothes specially designed for his age or the special meals or preferential treatment. At a very young age he would have been expected to take on simple tasks on the six acres, such as bird scaring or scouring the soil for missed potatoes. He would have had to help with the spinning or run errands. At night he would have slept with his parents or with all the other children because there was nowhere else and that was normal and, in winter, it was the only way to keep warm. He would have gone to bed, like all his family, in the few rags he wore all day. He wouldn't have needed a teddy for comfort because he had his brothers and sisters to cuddle.

Did Patrick go to school? He probably did as we believe he could read and write in later life, but it is unlikely he went to school near Knockatogher as he would have been too young before the family moved away.

Young goat herd.   Digging potatoes.

The 1841 census recorded that only 26 per cent of people over the age of five in Loughrea could read and write, and 11.5 per cent could read only. The number of children in school had trebled between 1800 and 1824, and boys like Patrick benefitted most from this so it could be that up to a half of young men could read. When Patrick was of school age he probably attended a Hedge School, so called because they were run by travelling teachers who set up schools in abandoned houses, sheds, and even under hedges because this education was illegal. Teachers ran the risk of punishment if they were caught because they were teaching the Catholic faith, although by the time Patrick went to school in, say, 1824 much of this repression had lost its severity. The standard of teaching varied enormously as teachers could be former seminarians, educated abroad, who could teach Latin and Greek or former Hedge School pupils who could barely get across the three Rs. These schools were funded by the parents if they could afford it and by collections held after Catholic church services.

This subject touches on the heart of how people thought in those days. Today we live in a so-called enlightened age in which a fact is not the truth unless someone can prove it by observation or repeatable experiment. In the early 1800s it was believed that God was greater than man, and if He, through a priest or the Bible, said something was true, then it was. So education, as instruction for life, was based on reading, writing, and Christianity—but which brand of Christianity? Education throughout Britain was aimed at encouraging the Protestant faith, and no Catholic was allowed to be a schoolmaster. This hurt people most of all in Ireland, in places like Knockatogher where the Catholic faith was the core of daily existence.

Father Dennis Madden was the Catholic priest in the parish of Kiltullagh-Killimordally from 1795 to 1825, the time when our Lally family lived in Knockatogher. He would have baptised Patrick and his brothers and sisters and maybe married James Lally and Annie Brett. He would certainly have been involved in the aftermath of the tragic events of July 1821. The old chapel in Kiltullagh was in ruins following over a century of suppression of Catholicism so he held services in fields or at crossroads. A major part of life for our families would have been Catholic religious observance, including constant references to the blessings of the many saints, each being the patron of some aspect of life.

An illicit mass in the fields.

Conversation would have been full of prayers for deliverance such as 'if the dear Lord wills it', which would be affirmed by 'God bless his holy name' from others and 'amen' from all. Attendance at Mass would be an important Sunday event, services often going on all day with crowds milling about between services gossiping, eating, and drinking. And everywhere would be hordes of children. Saint's Days would involve festivals such as dressing of holy wells or local pilgrimages to pray for particular needs to relevant patron saints. Holy wells, from which came blessed water, would always be worth a detour. The holy well in Kiltullagh was dedicated to St John the Baptist in 1714 by the owner of Kiltullagh House. His prayers to St John at the well reversed his fortunes in a chess match on which he had gambled the house, so a plaque was erected to this effect. This would have been enough for many people to plead to St John on this spot and expect a result. Later, a small boy fell into the well and drowned, and his spirit was said to wander the immediate area looking for small boys to take as companions, so little Patrick would never have been allowed near the well.

A holy well.

Do not smile at this story, as it was a serious part of the life of our Lally family and illustrates that the way they thought is difficult for many of us to comprehend now. Their life depended on nature, and all the seasons were celebrated. On the evening before May Day, flowers were picked, made into garlands, and spread around doors and windows to offer luck and keep the fairies out because they could never pass such sweet smelling flowers. There was a whole hierarchy of fairies, leprechauns, and banshees, good and bad, each of whom affected lives in different ways. Belief in these was normal, and many people claimed to have seen them.

Coming down to earth, the other major factor in the lives of the peasantry was their landlord. He was normally a Protestant, and they were Catholics. He could treat them as he saw fit. The Lally's landlord was James Daly, Lord Dunsandle, who lived in the largest house in the area named Dunsandle. It was situated a couple of miles south of Knockatogher, and its grounds, gardens, and nurseries extended to nearly the same area as the whole townland of Knockatogher. Lord Dunsandle was the Member of Parliament for the County of Galway and dominated the Galway City Corporation.

He was generally unpopular but was a powerful man who, it seems, suffered no opposition. He was particularly notorious for his suppression, conviction, and hanging of 'Ribbonmen' who protested for better rights for the poor and for Catholics and who, in the early 1820s, carried out a number of 'outrages', particularly in the east of County Galway, too near to Dunsandle for his Lordship's comfort. Our Lallys would have been in the thick of this, but we may never know if they took part. Lord Dunsandle was eventually ousted from power in November 1830, an event joyously recorded in *Freemans Journal*, the major Irish national newspaper:

Mr James Daly has been permitted by the independent electors of the county of Galway to retire and indulge in his rural recreations at Dunsandle, they having magnanimously eased him of the trouble of sitting in Parliament as the representative of this great county. This circumstance augers well for the cause of liberty and justice. The people of Galway have, therefore, reason to rejoice—the enfranchisement of whose merchants and tradesmen, if they be true to themselves, will serve as a final extinguisher to the lingering existence of Daly's corporation which has so long been the bane of their commercial prosperity and independence, the source of division and discord and the very slough of corruption.

So we leave little Patrick and his family as they move from Knockatogher to where they seem to have had a comparatively good living on their six acres, until that dreadful day. A comparatively good living was by no means easy, and we should not fool ourselves into believing that our family had never gone to bed hungry. Did they leave under pressure after the murders? Did they move to better things, or were they 'out on the street'?

3. Patrick Lally's Life in Ireland

By 1825 our family had left Knockatogher and was lost in the unrecorded mass of Irish peasantry in the Loughrea area. We must make much broader assumptions as to how they lived, but this gives us the opportunity to look in general at how all the Irish lived at this time and in particular how this affected Patrick as he grew up.

We have our picture from the census and the newspaper report of how Patrick lived in 1821. In terms of wealth, if that word can be used, the Lally family was about in the middle of the poverty-stricken Irish Catholic working class, farming six acres. He then re-appears in 1848 in London as a gardener and in charge of Lord Bruce's house. From about the age of ten in 1828 he would have had to be fully earning his keep. In looking at his life in these twenty years, let's look first at the main town in the area in which he lived, Loughrea, which was the commercial centre of the whole area.

Loughrea was one of the largest country towns in Connaught. It sat in the middle of a beautiful and fertile vein of land of low, rolling hills, running from the southwest around Gort to the northeast at Ballinasloe. Here were arable and livestock farms to a greater extent than elsewhere, particularly around Loughrea and Ballinasloe. There were also a large number of nurseries, market gardens, and large houses because of the pleasant countryside and climate. If we take a look at a semicircle north of Loughrea, extending out about eight miles to include Kiltullagh, Knockatogher, and Cappataggle, the area in which our family may have resettled, there were over forty large houses and estates, most with gardens and extensive kitchen gardens.

I think it's safe to picture young Patrick in Ireland as a gardener in one of these large houses or nurseries. This is where he learnt his known skills and also gained the confidence to deal direct with a lord in London or his estate manager. Maybe he left Ireland with a written reference. In this case he would have been employed back home and would not have depended on growing a few potatoes on a small plot and may have had a more mixed diet as one of the perks, official or not, of the job. He would, perhaps, have been given accommodation but this may only have been provided for single men and may explain the fact that he didn't marry while in Ireland. His father James' job as a publican also suggests that, although he depended on the spending power of his customers, he was not one of the masses directly dependant on the harvest and the whim of an agricultural landlord. All these are assumptions but, if true, show that the Lally family were lucky to be able to support themselves well until the fabric of society and all means of support crumbled away.

The town of Loughrea was situated next to a large lake, Lough Rea, meaning 'the grey lake', with a circumference of five miles, although there was no real frontage onto the lake, no promenade, and little industry related to it. It was a long town, east to west, with Main Street running along the middle on which nearly all the retailers were situated. Barrack Street, running parallel and nearer the lake, contained businesses such as attorneys, architects, and auctioneers as well as blacksmiths, shoe makers, a tannery, etc. It was a market town owned by Earl Clanricarde, the largest landowner in County Galway. His activities and those of his land agent dominated the local press because of the great effect they had on the local population. He is shown as being the immediate lessor of a third of the buildings and, through sublets, many more. These included the Town Hall, the police station and barracks, and army barracks, holding substantial forces of each, several large houses outside the town, and other notable buildings in it. He was responsible for appointing the Seneschal or town governor, coroners, and other town officials. His Court House was erected in 1821, and sessions were held there twice a year and, significantly, a court for the recovery of debts met once a week. The office of the regional revenue police was in Loughrea. A new handsome church with a fine steeple was also built in 1821 and the Catholic Chapel, 'a commodious structure with a tower containing one bell', and a Carmelite nunnery were rebuilt in 1829. So Loughrea seemed successful and growing in this period. Other main buildings included a bridewell, or small prison, and a Linen Hall, which had flourished when Loughrea was the main centre for trading linen and a poor quality coarse fabric called frieze.

The town's population nearly doubled between 1800 and 1840, from about 3,000 to about 5,500, in line with overall growth in the Irish population. Loughrea was still not a large town, yet *Pigot's Directory* of 1824 gave the town about sixty retailers and by 1846 *Slater's Directory* gave it over one hundred. The number of its businesses was based on serving a large area, perhaps up to ten miles round about, not just the population of the town itself, and it sat on the main route from Dublin to the west. The haberdashers, drapers, ironmongers, boot makers, even a clockmaker, would have served the gentry and attempted to stay up with the fashions of Dublin and London.

There was a busy market every Thursday for linen and provisions of all kinds; a smaller one on Saturday; and four fairs a year on saint's days when all sorts of animals were sold, particularly pigs. These markets would have attracted crowds. Main Street had well-built brick and stone buildings, including two banks, which can only suggest that Loughrea was a significant trading town and regional centre. The presence of three hotels would support this, and there were about

Scenes in a town like Loughrea.

twenty public houses with probably other premises serving beer in their front room. Loughrea also had a rare dispensary or clinic, not that the great majority of the townsfolk could afford to take advantage of it, and the only hospital in the county was in the city of Galway, twenty miles to the west.

There was little industry in Ireland at this time and the decline of linen manufacture left Loughrea's bakers, soap and candle makers, blacksmiths, coachbuilders, a printer, and farm-machinery repairers—all small businesses for local trade—at the heart of the commercial economy. The biggest factories were a brewery, two tanneries, and two corn mills in the town, all built in the 1830s.

Clearly there were some in Loughrea who had prospered, and on a pleasant day in the 1820s and 1830s Patrick could stroll the grounds of the Carmelite Abbey and the pleasant Abbey Walks overshadowed by lofty trees and view the ruins of the old abbey. But would Patrick have recognised these descriptions that come from contemporary guides and directories designed as much for pleasing local advertisers as for encouraging and enlightening the early nineteenth-century traveller? Just as today's guides to Asia, Africa, or South America describe their hotels and beauty spots but turn a blind eye to the slums, ghettos, and street children, so it was then in Loughrea.

By the 1820s Loughrea was showing real signs of decline, partly, it was claimed by local people, due to neglect by the young absentee earl and his agent but also due to the general decline in business and the economy. There was said to be nothing to attract people to the town except the regular fairs. A few new prominent buildings in the town and a rapidly increasing population were not necessarily signs of economic growth and well-being. As we have seen, the Linen Hall, even by 1824, was in a 'wretched state of neglect and decay'. The state of most houses was very bad, only the main street was

Going to market.

partly paved and there was very little in the way of sanitation. In that respect Loughrea differed little from many other towns throughout Britain, but in September 1838 even the *Galway Advertiser* printed the following description by a traveller:

> *'Loughrea is a very old town and towns in general are among the few things which improve with age. But Loughrea is a most ugly exception to this observation. It contains a beautiful ruin of an abbey, but the ruins of malt houses, corn stores and other modern edifices, in which it abounds, are unsightly in themselves and impart a sensation of dreariness and poverty which is very disagreeable.'*

If major works and prominent businesses were in 'ruins' you can be sure that houses of the inhabitants were worse. In 1842 *The Scenery and Antiquities of Ireland* described the suburbs of Loughrea as

> *'among the poorest and dirtiest now to be found in Ireland.'*

The Parliamentary Gazetteer of 1844 described the town in this way:

> *'The principal street is long, comparatively spacious and possessed of a large aggregate of tolerably good houses; yet in spite of its extent, its bustle and its somewhat urban aspect, it totally fails to relieve the town from a prevailing character of dinginess, dirtiness and neglect.'*

Patrick's story seems to be entwined with two of the largest landlords in Connaught; the arrogant Lord Dunsandle at Knockatogher and the earls of Clanricarde whose influence, whether of support or neglect, dominated life in the Loughrea area. The thirteenth Earl of Clanricarde was a relatively benevolent landlord who took a pride in the town, which thrived during his lifetime. He was a Protestant and his wife was a

Catholic, born at Marble Hill, eleven miles south of Loughrea. He died in 1808, and his six-year-old son inherited.

The fourteenth earl, born in 1802 in Hampshire, spent his early childhood at the family seat at Portumna, eighteen miles to the south east of Loughrea, but was educated at Eton and Oxford. When he reached his majority in 1823 a great celebration was held in his honour in Manahan's Hotel, Loughrea. He did not attend as he was celebrating in England. The report of the event in *The Connaught Journal* shows that the best of Loughrea society attended, but I cannot help but feel that their main motivation was to ingratiate themselves to the young lord as they cannot have failed to notice that the town was falling into decay.

In 1825 the earl married the daughter of George Canning who became British foreign secretary and briefly prime minister in 1827. On his marriage his Irish title was raised from Earl to Marquis of Clanricarde, and a year later he became Baron Somerhill in the English peerage giving him a seat in the British House of Lords. In 1838 he spent three years in St Petersburg as British ambassador to Russia. He was lord lieutenant of County Galway from 1831 until his death in 1874. I could go on, but I think the picture is clear. He was a very important man with many duties to take his eye off his Irish estates covering 57,000 acres, and off the lives of his poverty-stricken tenants.

From 1808, when his father died, until 1823, when he came of age, the Clanricarde estates were managed by an agent, Robert D'Arcy, who took most of the blame for the actions of that time. But it was after 1823 that the real decline of the town took place, and Clanricarde was not often there and he took no interest in the town itself. Several meetings were held in the late 1830s to try to discuss the reversal of Loughrea's decline and other grievances such as evictions. D'Arcy was often brave enough to attend despite vehement criticism, and in 1839 the marquis himself met a delegation from the town to discuss the reversal of its decline but took no action. He believed that the problems of Ireland could be solved by land reform and by emigration. He advanced these two ideas by putting a surcharge on new leases and renewals, which effectively evicted tenants from small plots in order to create larger, viable units. No new tenancy was given on plots of less than fifteen acres so tenants of smaller plots had to go. If our Lally family still had a small plot of about six acres and it was on Clanricarde land, this policy would have threatened and overshadowed their lives.

On the other hand, Clanricarde was in favour of Roman Catholic emancipation. He made generous donations to the Catholic Church, to the endowment of Maynooth College, the largest seminary in Ireland, to the building of Catholic churches on his estates, and to many other Catholic causes. He supported the legalisation of the payment of Catholic priests and gave the land for the new Boys' National School in 1832.

Loughrea was a busy town, and at any time of day there would have been people walking about doing business and chatting. It was busy but not hurried. Life in all of Ireland went at a leisurely pace, and there was always time to stand and talk. The *Guides* said that Loughrea had 'Society', meaning that there were important, knowledgeable people there worth meeting, with whom one could share news, opinions, business, and leisure. The presence of so many government offices, court, police, and army barracks meant that Loughrea had a higher than average Protestant population because they would have held all the main positions in these organisations.

There were several other organisations active and holding meetings in Loughrea, mainly for these society people:

lawyers, resident priests, and gentry living in the town and in the many large houses around Loughrea. Many of these notables were related, and they led lives totally divorced from those of the masses and revolving around the shared economic necessity of keeping their estates secure and in their families. They met at social events, weddings, grand balls, foxhunting, and horse racing.

The local horse-racing track was at Kiltullagh on land owned by Lord Dunsandle, and in 1839 Lord Dunsandle was a founder member of the new County of Galway Foxhounds.

The businesses in Loughrea that developed to serve these people set the town apart from many other towns in Connaught which were purely agricultural, labouring communities. Society people would have used the Irish coinage, which was different from the English coinage until 1826, but trade among the great majority of people was hand-to-mouth and almost entirely by barter of goods or services. The masses would have been familiar with coins but would seldom have had any and probably didn't trust them.

The day-to-day activities that Patrick would have seen in Loughrea would have included the arrival of the coaches that ran daily from Galway, Ennis, Gort, or Ballinasloe, but it was the upper classes who would have used them. The most numerous of the passenger carrying coaches were Bianconi's Coaches or 'Bians', as they were known. Carlo Bianconi had, from 1815, built a national business running routes linking all the major towns and cities in Ireland. The roads to the east of Loughrea were treacherous and unreliable as they travelled over deep bog land. In the frequent wet weather the going was very slow, and coaches could sink up to the carriage doors in mud.

Bianconi's cars or 'Bians'—a 'four horse car' and
a 'two horse day car'.

After fifty years of success and failure the Grand Canal was finally completed between Dublin and the River Shannon in 1804, and the Bians in Connaught acted as feeders to the canal, en route to Dublin carrying passengers, freight, and mail. In 1828 an extension canal was completed on the west of the River Shannon, to Ballinasloe, fifteen miles to the east of Loughrea. This extension took over two years to complete because nearly all the route was on shaking bog across which it was hardly possible to walk. Its building provided rare employment in activity other than agriculture. The canals ended the relative isolation of Connaught from the prosperous and fashionable life in Dublin because, unlike English canals, the Irish system was built mainly for passenger traffic. The seventy-six-mile canal journey from Ballinasloe normally took three days, but in the 1840s, with the threat of competition from the railway, new 'Swift Passage Boats' or 'Flys' were introduced. These managed the seventy-six miles in as little as eleven hours, using a team of four, frequently changed, galloping horses. The cost of the Bian from Loughrea to Ballinasloe was 2/-(10p) and a seat in the State Saloon of a Fly boat was 11/6 (58p). Both coaches and boats were busy and successful but only a small minority of the population could afford such a price.

Among the masses, a frequent topic of conversation was emigration and there was a steady stream of poor people leaving all through the early nineteenth century. Emigration was part of the way of life. Against the renting of an acre or two of harsh hillside or bog at home lay the prospect of owning a hundred acres in, say, America. Against the leaving of parents, family, and friends forever lay the prospect of offering your children a life free from poverty, hunger, and prejudice. For family-focused people these were hard decisions, but nearly all of those who found the money to go would have gone by canal as the only practical way of getting to Dublin. No State

Saloon for them. They would probably have gone by cart to Ballinasloe and then on the overcrowded slow canal boat with their one permitted bag each.

* * *

'Here or There, or Emigration a Remedy' from Punch, 1848.
It compares Irish life on the left with a happy family round a full table in a new land on the right.

Although the language of business and government was English, the voices all around Patrick would have been speaking Gaelic, which was the language used by the great majority in the West. The masses were unfamiliar with English and could perhaps only speak enough to take instructions from their employers and landlords. Most of the people Patrick would have met would have been dressed in smocks of homemade frieze, the cheap linen cloth. Women wore flannel jackets and petticoats generally of blue or dark red. In the winter the men often wore homemade shoes and socks while most women and children went barefoot all year round.

Although transport for the majority was on foot, and many would never in their lifetime travel more than a day's walk from home, the streets were full of donkeys and carts most of which, by the 1840s, would have had wooden spoke wheels as the old solid wood wheeled carts were gradually dying out. And, of course, the mail and passenger coaches with two or four horses arrived almost hourly.

The coaches also brought the newspapers, but few were sold. In the 1820s *The Connaught Journal* was said to have a circulation of 192 copies and *Connolly's Weekly Advertiser* 145 copies. Neither newspaper was printed in Loughrea. National newspapers printed perhaps 500 or 600 copies and some titles eventually reached Loughrea from England. Readership was a lot larger than circulation because the newspapers were passed round or read to a group of listeners on a street corner. A Temperance Reading Room opened in 1840 with a library of newspapers and books to cultivate a thirst for knowledge.

The Temperance Movement, which flourished for a few years at this time in Ireland, gives a good illustration of everyday life in Loughrea. *The Tuam Herald* reported on 7 December 1839 that 'upwards of 200 of the most notorious drunkards' have left Loughrea to visit Fr. Theobald Mathew, the great teacher of teetotalism, who had recently visited the town. One has to wonder how many drunkards there were in a town of 5,000. On Good Friday in 1840, 1,000 members of the Loughrea Temperance Society marched through the town waving flags and ribbons, following the Temperance Band. Over that Easter more than 2,000 'took the pledge' to abstain from alcohol. This number must surely have included many from outside the town and shows how Loughrea acted as a centre for activities of people living all around. Was Patrick one of the notorious drunkards or one of those who took the pledge? Certainly in later life he was amongst the former and this may have been why several of his children were involved in the Temperance Movement in London sixty years later.

Loughrea had its share of political activity too. In the 1820s and 1830s several groups of agitators for agrarian reform were active in the area, attacking the property of landlords and harming their animals. The most active and violent of these were the 'Terry Alts', a group that arose in County Clare, spreading north to the Loughrea area and reaching the peak of its activities after the failure of the potato crop in 1830. In May 1831, the escalating number of murders and an attack on Marble Hill, the main residence of the Burke family and childhood home of Lord Clanricarde's mother, brought about a crackdown. Later that year twenty-one agitators were condemned to death and a further ninety eight jailed or deported.

Patrick Lally, even at the age of twelve or thirteen, would have been well aware of these major local events. Daniel O'Connell, who dominated Irish political life in the 1830s with his campaigns for Catholic emancipation held one of his 'monster meetings' in Loughrea in September 1843, choosing the town because it was a key centre convenient to all his supporters from miles around. This meeting attracted 30,000 'Repealers' and supporters who gathered in the town and, led by the Temperance Band, processed to, what was described by the press reporter as, 'a green and pleasant eminence in full view of several houses of Tory opponents'. Here O'Connell addressed the crowd in constant torrential rain. This would have been one of the biggest events in Loughrea's history, but was Patrick a member? Had he paid his farthing a week, penny a month, shilling a year? As a young man Patrick would have had to have an opinion. He would either have been there or been one of the few who deliberately stayed away. *Freeman's Journal* frequently printed interminable lists of new members and activists in the Repeal Movement and lists a James Lally and a Patrick Lally but, as Dublin tailors, these are unlikely to have been our ancestors. When Patrick reached London he could have joined one of the active Repeal branches there.

Torrential rain was commonplace. Normally Loughrea had twice as much rain as London, but as it fell in heavy downpours on fewer days more days were dry and the Irish were always ones to count their blessings. And because the weather came straight off the Atlantic, Loughrea had half the rain of the west of County Galway. The temperature was even with few really cold winters and few very hot days in summer—a lot to be thankful for. Torrential rain didn't seem to bother the locals who were used to it. They stood out, soaked, carrying on their business or conversations, the ladies perhaps wrapping their shawls over their heads in an attempt to keep off the worst of it. The men would pull down their flower pot hats a bit tighter and carry on calmly.

Hurricanes were a lot less common, but in 1839 the 'Night of the Big Wind' visited catastrophe on the town, adding more heavy burdens to Loughrea's people and changing the landscape for a lifetime. The Great Wind occurred on the night of 6 and 7 January 1839 and started with an unnatural calm and a dramatic rise in temperature that afternoon. By the evening there was an oppressive dense atmosphere full of foreboding. The wind hit at nine o'clock in the evening accompanied by whirlwind after whirlwind. In Loughrea over 100 houses were completely destroyed, most by fire started when chimneys came down and the sparks from fires set light to the thatch. Hardly a building in the town was undamaged, many having their flimsy thatch blown away. About 600 people were made homeless.

For Loughrea and surrounding countryside, already suffering severe neglect, this was a terrible set-back, which could never be fully rectified. Churches and large country houses all suffered. Nobody can know how many hovels out in the country were blown away and with them went hay, whole flocks of chickens, small animals, and crops stored outside or in damaged barns. Many animals were killed by falling trees as they tried to shelter. Torrential rain caused dreadful flooding. Every tree on the Abbey Walks was toppled causing much damage as they came down. It is estimated that two million trees fell in Ireland in that one night so the landscape was made more bleak and bare. Many church steeples came down. Five miles away at Craughwell the trees were covered in salt from sea spray blown fifteen miles inland, and in large areas drinking water was salty. There were tales of fish falling from the sky. Not a family was unaffected.

A disaster like this was not considered a random extreme event of nature. It had to have its reasons. Those blamed ranged from fairies who were believed to have a night of revelry every fifth of January, the feast of St. Ceara, to freemasons who Catholics believed to be associated with demonic practices, which had got out of control. The storm was also on the night of the Epiphany when Christ made himself known to the world and on which many believed He would come again. So Loughrea was a very shaken town, physically and emotionally. People were very frightened. Something was very wrong in the world.

After the immediate damage came a doubling of food prices not only because of this loss of crops but also because hardly a road was passable due to the fallen trees. A relief fund was set up, as were many all over Ireland, and many generous donations were made but only enough to help those worst affected. Lady Clanricarde gave £20 and the money raised from the sale of the timber from felled trees which came to about another £40. A donation eventually came from the Marquis of Clanricarde who was in Russia, but his £5 was considered derisory and no better than that given by many of the local gentry.

* * *

If we were to have asked Patrick what his family and friends did in their leisure time, I fear it would be a question he would not have understood. Life was not rigidly divided into work and play. As we will see, the great majority dined only on potatoes, which did not require all a family's time and effort to grow. There was none of today's nine-to-five regularity. Patrick would not have had a watch or clock. His work would have consisted of digging and planting in the spring, earthing up the plants during the summer, and harvesting in the autumn. So there was plenty of time to sing, dance, drink, and play the fiddle. Neighbours would crowd into houses in the winter or meet at crossroads or a village in the summer to enjoy themselves. Wakes, weddings, and religious festivals were regular reasons for a party, and a horse race or fight would draw great crowds. The twenty public houses in Loughrea served mainly beer and whiskey, but unlicensed whiskey was made in great quantities everywhere. Many drank poteen, a potent firewater made from barley or potatoes. Whole families would think nothing of walking many miles to a fair and certainly our Lallys would have been in Loughrea for the fairs, particularly the two day fair on 26 and 27 May when, if they'd walked in from the country, they would have slept in a crowded barn or under a hedge during the night. The image of the happy-go-lucky Irish was true in those days and they carried their cares lightly

Everybody knew everybody and just talking was a major activity. Every stranger was welcome and would be engaged in conversation and offered a meal and somewhere to lie down.

No matter how little they had, it was shared. The Irish were well mannered, honest, and in normal circumstances always to be trusted. A young lady could walk alone without fear and be engaged in conversation by strangers who, despite having had little education, often showed remarkable native knowledge and familiarity with traditional tales and classical texts, which they may have heard round a fireside and remembered. Storytelling was a great oral tradition, and not having any books, the typical Irishman developed a great memory for every detail in stories and events. This is how Patrick would have heard and remembered the stories he told later.

We have looked at the education Patrick may have received in the country, but in the town of Loughrea there were several schools. After the relaxation of the penal laws in 1782 several private schools were set up, and sixteen were listed in Loughrea in 1826. In that year attendance totalled 832 in Loughrea, but a child could only attend if his parents could pay at least something towards the cost. Most of these schools were single rooms in the master's house, usually in an appalling state of disrepair. Equipment was in very short supply. There was a mix of ages and abilities and no control on the ability of the master or mistress. Learning was often by rote with little understanding.

Education throughout Britain was aimed at encouraging the Protestant faith. No Catholic was allowed to be a school teacher, and this hurt most keenly in Ireland. Classes were always in English, partly because nearly every suitable book was published in English, but also because Gaelic was considered by the authorities to be a primitive language not worth learning. It must have been difficult for a poor Irish child to learn a new language if he couldn't practice it at home.

There was one free 'Charter' school for poor girls of Loughrea, but at the end of their education the girls were apprenticed to a

Protestant master and this limited the number of Catholics who wanted their children taught there. Of the twenty-five books used at the school, nineteen were religious works and tracts such as *Seeker's Lectures and Sermons Against Popery* and six related to spelling, reading, and arithmetic. So education can't have been a lot of fun. In 1831 a new national system of free education in non-denominational schools was introduced with religious education left to priests outside school hours. As Patrick was thirteen then, he would have missed any benefits this may have brought, but our three Lally girls, born about 1835, may have been able to take advantage of it, as in 1837 there were 1,200 children in school in Loughrea. Although the structure of education itself was not a lot different from that in England at the time, the fact that the religion and language of education was not that of the mass of the population meant it was less effective, and in Patrick's time even fewer parents in Ireland could afford it. So it is not surprising that, in the 1840s, fewer than half the men in Loughrea could even sign their signature on their marriage register compared with two thirds who could do so in England. But Patrick did so.

Irish beggars.

4. The Real Hard Facts of Irish Life

So this was the environment in which the Lallys lived near Loughrea, but many contemporary government and independent reports allow us to look a lot deeper to find how the Irish really lived. These reports and statistics paint the background of the lives of our family from about 1825.

By the 1830s the Irish economy was grinding to a halt. Most industry had gone, agricultural prices had collapsed, and, more and more, every tier of society depended on people scratching a living growing potatoes on a tiny piece of land. The potato crop frequently failed, and people starved. Then they couldn't pay the rent so the landlord suffered too. Even the apparently rich had little ready money as their capital was tied up, and they lived on debt. Despite this debt many continued to live lavish lifestyles well beyond their means. It was from Ireland that many an early nineteenth century traveller returned declaring that the poverty was the worst they had seen in Europe. In 1839 Frenchman, Gustave de Beaumont wrote:

> 'In all countries paupers may be discovered, but an entire nation of paupers is what never was seen until it was shown in Ireland.'

It seems that our Lally forebears were in the middle of this nation of paupers. I have made assumptions that Patrick was better off than many, but even so he would have gone hungry frequently and would have been surrounded by the politics and the discrimination of the time and the poverty and starvation of other family members and friends, perhaps even his employers.

The potato was a basic food of millions of people all over Britain and Europe. Provided the crop didn't fail, the potato allowed enormous quantities of nutritious food to be produced from small plots with little effort. Growing potatoes required no skill and no tools other than a spade. They didn't need to be ground before eating. They produced five times the nutrition from a patch of land than did grains, so in good years they result in a fit and healthy population. In the early nineteenth century, potatoes were a key reason for the dramatic growth in the Irish population. The potato, occasionally boiled with milk, compared very favourably with the basic bread and cheese diet of the English agricultural labourer. The difference In Ireland, however, was the almost total dependence on this one crop. In Connaught 70 per cent of the population ate only potatoes, and 80 per cent of all food eaten was potato. Many people had never tasted anything else. Grains such as corn, wheat, oats, and barley were grown in Ireland, particularly in the fertile valley around Loughrea, but nearly all were exported because they travelled easily and got a better price in England. Few in Ireland had the money to buy grains at any price, and they lived a hand-to-mouth existence, eating their own potatoes from their own plot.

But potatoes do not keep, as do grains. Typically a family living off a few acres would put their potatoes in a pit to last them all year. Should there not be enough or if they rotted and the family ran out in, say, June, the family would starve or take to the roads begging. They might buy in grain at an exorbitant price from a usurious dealer who would come round later demanding his money and probably taking some of next year's potato crop as payment. They would promise him 4d for a stone (6.4 kilograms) of potatoes rather than pay 1½d or 2d. This is why the months of June, July, and August were often called the meal months when meal had to be eaten at great cost. There was little other work that needed to be done between sowing and harvesting and no other employment that might bring them additional income to tide them over. Because they had no money or cash income they usually paid rent by working the fields of their landlord and that brought them no income from which to pay to feed themselves in hard times.

Hunger was a part of life and starvation a frequent occurrence. A previous major famine in 1741 and 1742 led to the death of 25 per cent of the Irish population. The years we are looking at started with a partial failure in 1800 and another, due to frost, occurred in 1807. In 1821 and 1822 the potato crop failed completely in Connaught, and the first charitable subscriptions were raised in England to counter the 'distress, horrible beyond description' that occurred. These complete failures of the potato crop were after Patrick was born in 1818. The years 1830 and 1831, when Patrick was twelve, saw total failure in many parts including Galway, and 1838 and 1840 were the only good crop years in the twelve years from 1832 to 1844.

The whole local population, trapped in a dependence on the potato, experienced this deprivation. Even if, as we are assuming, Patrick was not directly affected by the loss of his personal crop, he would have suffered along with everybody else. *The Illustrated London News* of June 1842 describes scenes that demonstrate people's desperation: the raiding of potato and oat stores in Galway and Loughrea by hungry, rioting mobs. Not only was food short but traders were buying up what was offered for sale and hoarding it to force prices up further. The 1842 harvest was an average one but had yet to be gathered in so June was the start of the meal months and people were hungry.

* * *

Class 2. A good farm or town house.

Class 3. A mud brick house.

We have noted the sort of house in which Patrick and his family lived in 1821, but we must depend on general descriptions to assess what their house was like later. The census of 1841 placed 'houses' in four classes described thus with their percentages as recorded in Connaught.

1. Less than 1 per cent — Large houses.
2. 9 per cent — Good farm or town house with five to nine rooms and windows with glass.
3. 38 per cent — Mud brick house with one or two rooms, open windows.
4. 53 per cent — Mud cabin with one room, no windows or chimney.

Clearly the house of the Lally family in 1821 fell into the third (38 per cent) class. The fourth class was described by another foreign traveller as being:

Of dried mud and built with walls the height of a man. The roofs of these dwellings were made of thatch so old that the grass which covered it could be confused with the neighbouring meadows. In more than one place I saw the flimsy timbers supporting these fragile roofs had yielded to the effects of time, giving the whole thing the effect of a mole hill on which a passer-by had trod. The houses mostly had neither windows nor chimneys; the daylight came in and the smoke went out by the door. If one could see into the houses, it was rare to notice more than bare walls, a rickety stool and a small peat fire burning slowly and dimly between four flat stones.

(Alexis de Tocqueville, 1836)

Class 4. Three mud cabins.

In Connaught between 40 per cent and 60 per cent of the population lived in this lowest, fourth class. The 60 per cent level probably dominated in the more rocky and marshy farmland to the west, and in the better off Loughrea area it was probably 40 per cent. Many of these so-called houses had holes in the roof to let the smoke out, but this would also let the heat out and the rain in, even more than normal. There is also much evidence of a fifth class below these four. The census of 1841, which put the population of Ireland at 8.2 million, was generally considered a gross underestimate because no census enumerator had ventured far out into the bogs and mountains to count the evicted and unemployed barely managing to keep alive in caves, ditches, and under tree roots. These dwellings, if you can call them that, were known as scalps or, even worse, scalpeens. A sample study in County Clare, which borders Galway to the south, added 30 per cent to the total census population, many coming from this unrecorded lowest class.

Class 5. Scalps and scalpeens
out in the hills and bogs.

In September 1836 'The Report of The Poor Law Commissioners' on the state of the poor in Ireland was presented to Parliament. The commissioners had visited villages across Connaught speaking to groups of ordinary local people to get a true feel of the situation. They visited Kilchreest, a small village four miles south west of Loughrea, where they interviewed nineteen people ranging from farmer and priest to beggar and including John Lally, a nailer. The consensus was that this area was better off than other parts yet still it was reported that:

Judy Donnell's habitation under a bridge.

Many were obliged to pledge their clothes in the pawn office at Loughrea last July and were not able to go to mass for the want of them. (James McTighe, baker)

Their report from Ballina, eighty-five miles north of Loughrea, included results of a detailed survey carried out by the parish priest that showed what the poorer areas were like. It stated the main reason that the majority of children did not attend the free schools:

the rest being prevented, not by want of shoes, stockings, cap or bonnet, which here are scarcely thought of as part of a boy's or girl's dress, but by want of sufficient clothing to cover their nakedness and subject them to assemble without shocking decency.

55

His survey also covered the sleeping arrangements of his 10,553 parishioners. It is interesting that this priest with great local knowledge assumed that even those few people who could afford a bed slept three people in it:

> *In the whole parish there are 400 feather beds so that, supposing three persons to lie on each bed, 9,353 lie at best on straw. From a similar calculation it appears that 7,000 are sleeping on the floors of damp cabins . . . . Many have no blanket at all but sleep on the floor, having no covering but the rags they wear by day.*

For furniture there was almost none. It was a luxury to have a box to put anything in. Most had a cast-iron pot in which to boil potatoes and maybe a milk tub and a wicker basket. Bedding was straw and very few blankets laid on the damp mud floor. In 1837 a survey was carried out in Tullahobagly, County Donegal, a parish about the same size as Loughrea. It reported:

> *The inhabitants, numbering about 9,000, had only 10 beds, 93 chairs and 243 stools between them. Pigs slept with their owners, manure heaps choked doors, sometimes even stood inside; the evicted and unemployed put roofs over ditches, burrowed into banks, existed in bog holes.*

These descriptions of Ballina and Tullahobagly are extreme cases, but the Commissioners' report shows that the fertile lowland round Loughrea was relatively prosperous and the Lallys were probably not as totally poverty stricken as people in other areas, particularly further west. But all the other information on the houses and furniture of the inhabitants of Connaught is from government reports concerning the general state of Ireland and is not included for dramatic effect. We are trying to imagine how our ancestors lived, and even if the Lally house was in the third class of the four or five it sounds dreadful but would have given them a lot to be thankful for.

In middle-range cabins the whole family lived in the one room. Typically there were many children; twelve was not unusual. People married at a very young age, often as young as sixteen or seventeen, because there was nothing to stop them. They didn't need to save before the marriage because there was no money. They didn't need to build a career because the only job was to till the land. When they had to leave the house because there was no longer room for them, boys and girls got together for security and some home comforts.

This raises, of course, one of the big questions about Patrick. Why had he not married when he left Ireland in his late twenties? Could he have lost his job if he married? Could he afford to wait or did the death of a first wife drive him abroad? We can't guess and we'll probably never know.

A newly married couple often had no means of support, but they would find a bit of land to rent or move up to the hills to take over a new unused bit of poor rocky land. Often they would move on to a new cabin thrown up on the same piece of land as their parents or a piece of land nearby with no regard for their ability to pay the rent unless there was a good potato crop. There was nothing else they could do, and any of these options meant they could eat for at least one more year and worry about the rent then. And so the plots got smaller and smaller. In 1841 64 per cent of landholdings in Connaught were under the five acres that was considered the minimum to support a family. The landlord knew the tenant would be unable to pay but also knew that this would put him in a position in which he could legally evict the tenant and take his goods in lieu of rent: potatoes or perhaps grain or a pig.

These goods would often be sent to England for sale at a higher price than at home. The English then wondered how the Irish could be starving, as they so often heard, when so much good food was exported by them. Meanwhile the Irish did starve due to lack of food.

> *People starve in the midst of plenty, as literally as if dungeon bars separated them from a granary. When distress has been at its height, and our poor have been dying of starvation on our streets, our corn has been going to a foreign market. It is, to our own poor, a forbidden fruit.*
>
> *(Dr Dominic J Corrigan, On Famine and Fever as Causes and Effect in Ireland, Dublin 1846)*
>
> *Immense herds of cattle, sheep and hogs . . . floating off on every tide, out of every one of our thirteen seaports, bound for England; and the landlords were receiving their rents and going to England to spend them; and many hundreds of poor people had laid down and died on the roadside for want of food. (John Mitchell, Jail Journal or Five Years in British Prisons, New York 1854)*

The land the poor worked on, their plot, was also usually unimproved and derelict. Nothing was considered beyond that year's crop so perhaps some manuring was the only action taken to improve it. Manure became important in itself and was anxiously sought out but nothing else was done. This analysis is from a political pamphlet produced in about 1840:

> *A country naturally fertile is left almost unimproved and only half cultivated; the fields are undrained; the rivers, left without care, overflow their banks and turn good land into marsh; straggling hedges and uncultivated spots deform the face of the country; the hay or corn, insufficiently secured,*

is exposed to the weather and much land capable of culture is left to its natural wilderness or is so ill tilled that it is little better than waste.

(Alexander Somerville)

As we have seen, a family's existence was very dependent on the attitude of their landlord. Another traveller in Ireland in August 1838 pointed out the contrast possible from one area to the next, one landlord to the next. One of the areas he describes was owned by Lord Dunsandle who also owned Knockatogher and may demonstrate his attitude to all his tenants. This was reported in *The Morning Chronicle* of 12 September 1838 under the heading of 'Gleanings from the West of Ireland'. The newspapers of the day didn't mince their words.

Killyemore is a miserably neglected village with an excessive population in it and about it. It stands on the estate of Mr Daly of Dunsandle formerly member for Galway County and proprietor as he seemed to consider himself (for he did what he like with it) of Galway Borough. Mr Daly, having been relieved of the onerous duties of a parliamentary life by the people of the county and the responsibility of borough patronage by the reform bill has the more leisure to attend to the comforts of his own people upon his estates; and it is indeed a pity that he does not look after his shirtless and shoeless and roofless serfs here at Killyemore. They are said to belong immediately to a middleman who derives an interest under the head proprietor but that is not a fair way—albeit a very usual one—of shifting the responsibility entirely from the landlord. Why is there no school in Killyemore but such as the ragged paupers contrive among themselves to keep up? Wherefore is there no dispensary for providing medicine and advice for the sick? Why is the place entirely abandoned to the protection of the parish priest and the disinterested pity of two or three humane gentlemen living in the neighbourhood? Mr Daly is commonly reputed to be a good man . . . which makes the disgraceful condition of this portion of his estates the more remarkable.

Near this village is Bearnesbrook, a very fine place, which with the surrounding estate belonged to a Mr Hearne. He died young and unmarried leaving his estate to an only sister who married an officer of the Highland Regiment . . . The lady's choice was a happy one for the neighbourhood and doubtless even so for herself. Mr Kirkcaldy, having turned his claymore into a sickle devotes himself to the care of his property and gives every encouragement and assistance to his tenants in promoting a better and more profitable system of husbandry amongst them. He employs great numbers of the peasantry in the labour of his extensive farms and is extolled in the warmest terms for kind, benevolent and considerate conduct to all his neighbours. This is much better, in my humble opinion, than a Galway husband with half a dozen foxes' brushes nailed to the stable door, a coach and four like a moveable cigar divan filled within and without with rural dandies plying at all the regattas and watering places in the kingdom and one half-year's rent gone before the quarter of the next is due.

The last sentence is hardly complimentary of Lord Dunsandle, living beyond his means. There was so much complexity and contradiction in the Irish situation but this is the background to our family's life for more than twenty years after we saw them at Knockatogher. There are occasionally hints as to Lally families within our parishes around Loughrea, such as the Anne Lally who died in Cappataggle in 1837, but nothing that tells us for certain where our family was. They were there somewhere, among all this distress. Things were going to get worse and, in the twenty-first century when in Britain the state is obliged to step in when someone simply trips over a broken paving stone, you must be asking how such a dreadful situation could have arisen and how it was allowed to continue. We shall look at this next.

5. The Underlying Reasons for Irish Problems

The purpose of this story is to try to describe how our Lally ancestors lived—those who moved away from Loughrea in the 1840s and have, over several generations, brought you and me to where we are today. Perhaps now is the time to pause and look around at the room you're sitting in, your house, family, and neighbourhood and think over the dramatic differences in the lives being described and the life you live today. It is not my purpose to go into all the reasons for the state in which our Lally forbears existed but they do tell us more about our Lally lives in Loughrea. Many books have been written on this complex subject. They each state similar facts, but even they present contradictions over reasons and consequences and it would be impossible for me to give simple correct answers in a couple of pages. But now is the time to briefly touch on a few of these reasons. The consequences are already clear.

Among the penalties imposed upon Catholics after the Battle of The Boyne in 1690 was that they were prohibited from buying land and they were forced, on death, to distribute any land they owned equally among all their sons. Over more than a century and four or five generations the land had been broken up into small, uneconomic plots. Before 1650 Catholics had owned 60 per cent of all land. By 1780 this had dropped to 5 per cent and by the early 1800s Catholic land ownership was negligible. Until the Act of Union in 1801 even the legal position of Catholic priests was in doubt, and they had to act cautiously for fear of arrest. Even after relaxation of the most penal laws by 1801, Catholics could not have any but the most junior jobs in the civil service; they could not be judges or hold rank in the army or navy or sit in Parliament. Before then, Catholics were not allowed to build churches, and it was not until partial Catholic emancipation in 1829 that a Catholic chapel was erected in Loughrea.

The great, ruling Catholic families had been destroyed, and yet 95 per cent of the population was still Catholics. This is why every Catholic pauper or beggar regaled his listeners with tales of his lost inheritance and that he was 'a noble lord fallen on hard times'. It could well have been true! With their tradition of passing down stories around the fireside, and perhaps a little exaggeration, tales of just a few generations back would have been clear in their mind. Even the most lowly members of a clan had, in the old days, their status and place in society and could claim direct connection with the head of the clan himself, even if it was only, for example, that their aunt was married to the chief's cousin.

James Lally would have passed on to his son Patrick his links back to the great lords of Hy Maine in ancient times: the Lallys and Mulallys of Tollendal Castle near Tuam with the family motto 'Just and Valiant'. Their lands stretched south to cover the whole fertile valley around Loughrea. James' and Patrick's ancestor, Gerard Lally, was a representative at the Court of King James in 1689 but in 1690 fought for the Stuart cause and was outlawed and fled to France. The Lally lands were confiscated and given to the likes of the Burkes and Clanricardes to whom the Lallys may by the 1840s have been paying their rent. In France Gerard Lally's family married into French aristocracy and became the Counts of Lally Tollendal.

Gerard's son, Thomas Lally, became a famous French military commander, fighting the British in India in the 1760s. Thomas was hated by his own men because of his arrogance and cruelty, and it is ironic that, in India, he despised the native population and did his best to destroy their culture and religion. But he was on the Catholic Irish side and on the Lally side so all this could be overlooked. He may have been executed by the French in 1766, but he was posthumously reprieved twelve years later.

These were the great Lally heroes of not so long ago, at a time when the clan gave mutual support to all in times of trouble—when they belonged. There were still reports of the doings of the French Lally Tollendals in the press in the 1800s, but that was no help. All that family and tribal support was gone; they were totally demoralised and they now had nowhere to turn in their desperate poverty.

Catholic loyalties were very different to those of the British and Irish ruling Protestant classes. Catholics supported the Americans in their fight for independence from British rule in the 1780s. Their sympathies were with the Catholic countries of Europe, and many Irish Catholics actively supported the French in the war against Britain, even to the point of inspiring the French invasion in 1794, when only bad weather and poor leadership prevented a fleet carrying 14,000 men from landing on British soil in Ireland. So the British establishment looked on Irish Catholics as traitors. The Irish Catholics, who in their suppression could find no redress, equally despised the English invaders and overlords.

* * *

The excessive population of Ireland was recognised as a major contributor to its problems. Despite poverty and frequent food shortages, the population of Ireland had grown to 8.2 million in 1841 and, as we have seen, maybe more because the 1841 Ireland census may have been an underestimation. The population of England and Wales, by comparison, was less than double this figure, at 15.9 million. Many considered the Irish population to be unsustainable.

As the population grew, the land was divided, subdivided, and divided again through the generations, leaving plots smaller and smaller. There wasn't an economy, as such, that could offer employment, so if a landowner had five sons and had been allowed to leave his land to one, what would the other four have done? The actual tiller of the soil could pay his rent to a sub-landlord who paid it to another, and to another, so that it was not uncommon for a chain of eight so-called landlords each to take a fraction of the money that came from that one patch of land. Each was impoverished and desperate to pay the man above him for fear of eviction so may have turned viciously on the man below him to receive his money.

If a toiler improved his land, his rent would promptly be increased or he would be evicted in favour of someone who could pay more. No middle man would dream of improving his land, and the ultimate owner was too divorced from the whole situation. Boundaries were ill defined and open to dispute. Few leases could ever be upheld in court. So the complexity of tenancy and ownership meant that no land could be sold, and it often became a millstone around the necks of toilers, middlemen, and ultimate owners, whoever they were. The vicious circle was complete.

Even most members of what might here be called the upper classes were in debt; living beyond their means. Their expenditures included taxes, maintenance and living expenses, mortgages and debts from previous bad times, and, in many cases, 'portions' and annuities tied to the property by marriage settlements and wills of previous generations. The 'rich' landowner was legally obliged to pay all this from rental income from tiers of poverty-stricken sub-landlords and tenants, and there was no escape as their land was virtually worthless and unsaleable. Most estates were, in effect, bankrupt although nobody bothered to sue for their debt, because even if they won, there would be no money to pay them. It would only take a small thing for the whole system to collapse. And, of course, it did.

Most tenants lived in constant dreadful fear of their landlord and of eviction from their hovel and patch of land. Eviction frequently meant death. There was nowhere the tenant could go and nobody to act for him, as described by Alexander Somerville.

> *The enmity of Protestant and Catholic led the first, he being usually the landlord, to allow the latter, the potato eating tenant, to get in arrear, that he might at any time be evicted by means of the law when a better tenant offered for the land. The Protestant landlord, having all the law on his side—all officials being Protestant, from lord lieutenant to the hangman—he was seldom particular about the moral judgement of such cases. There were armed police ever at hand to help the landlord if the tenant did not yield possession and betake himself to a ditch to lie and die quietly. If he took vengeance into his own hand while in that ditch or behind the hedge that skirted it and the highway road there was the hangman for him; that is, if they could catch him and get the noose round his neck.*

There were also economic reasons for the problems of Ireland. In the eighteenth century Ireland was relatively successful and growing in agriculture and industry. James and Annie Lally would have experienced these good times in their early lives but would have then seen their reversal, particularly from about 1815

An ejectment.

The day after ejectment.

when the Napoleonic Wars ended. Ireland had good markets for its agricultural produce in North America, but by the early nineteenth century this had gone as colonists developed their own farmland. There was also a good market in England but after the end of the war against France in 1815 Britain was opened up to cheaper European supplies.

Prices of the key Irish exports, meat and grain, halved in the Dublin markets between 1812 and 1816 and never recovered. In the late 1700s Loughrea's linen industry had supported about 300 looms, mostly in the homes of outworkers and these were supplied by hundreds of flax spinners like our Lallys in Knockatogher. It is reported that in 1761 just one trader sent 55,000 yards of cloth to market in Dublin. By the 1830s this industry had disappeared from the area, the main reason being the perfection in 1790 in Leeds of the flax spinning machine and the gradual multiplying of huge mills in England employing hundreds of women producing vast quantities of regular, good-quality yarn and cloth at a price no Irish home worker could match with their home made spinning wheels and looms. Loughrea would also previously have benefitted from a thriving trade in wool and cotton. By 1815 this was also in real decline, again because failure to invest in new machinery made the quality and price unacceptable. The 1801 Act of Union provided for the phasing out of all duties and by 1824 Ireland had become a full part of Britain and free trade was the final blow to local industry. Cloths and any manufactured goods could be imported into Ireland more cheaply than could be made at home.

Imagine the effect of this on our family after 1821 when the moved on from Knockatogher. Throughout Patrick's life all he would have seen was decline in industry to virtually nothing by the 1840s. By the early 1830s the family income from flax spinning had gone. The population was still rising rapidly and this led to even more subdivision of land, and there were no factories they could move to as in England. Overall agricultural production increased slightly but didn't keep up with the number of mouths to feed, and if James Lally still had six acres, his produce would only get half the price at market in 1830 as it had in 1820. His only option would have been to live hand-to-mouth off his land, and that meant more and more dangerous dependence on potatoes that he could easily sow, gather, and eat. The price and population pressure was on landlords too. Their prices had halved; they had greater difficulty getting in the rents but they had more bills to pay than did James Lally.

Much of Loughrea's linen industry had been built up by Protestants from the north. The general opinion was that, if you wanted a job done, you brought in a Protestant to do it because they were more reliable, conscientious, and business-minded. Such an attitude would have been borne out by the relative prosperity of Protestant Ulster in the north. In the south, industry and trade were thought to be strangled by the Irish attitude of living only for the moment, never planning for the recurring bad times in the future.

Alexander Somerville reported on the situation in Ireland in 1847 for the *Manchester Examiner*. He grew up in poverty on a Scottish croft and was first employed as a labourer. This background enabled him to see all sides of the Irish problem better than most, as we shall see later too, but his two reports here show this Irish attitude to work and business:

> *'The higher classes of people have such a contempt for trade . . . . The poor people imitate them and will not trade unless compelled. When compelled to try a mercantile life in a small way they have no capital to begin with and consequently have no profits. If they do get a good return on some venture, they enjoy themselves and do not think of enlarging trade.'*

To build a business, to make a profit was seen as racketeering and one could be ostracised as working against the common good.

> *There has been frosty and snowy weather for ten days. Turf fuel is cut on the bogs, dried and piled up. It is brought in to this large village* by the people of the bogs in donkey carts and sold, a small cart load for sixpence. The money is expended on meal which is taken to the bogs, the men and asses famishing and the men telling the stranger how they starve; but as soon as they get out and have filled their bellies they will not stir to bring another load of turf into town until the stomachs can bear the hunger no longer. I asked some persons of consequence here why they or some one did not purchase a large store of turf in good weather and retail it to the poor in bad weather when, as is the case now, it cannot be procured from the bogs and people must go without fires . . . . They heard me with a kind of surprise approaching horror, to think that I should recommend the fuel of the poor creatures should be purchased up and sold at a profit.*
>
> (*On the banks of the Shannon so, I would guess, Portumna. SL)

We have to accept that these would have been the views of our Lally family at this time. The nation was ruined by a malaise of hopelessness or idleness, depending on your point of view. It is easy to see how hopelessness was brought on by the impossibility of making a living against a background of land confiscations, religious persecution, social disturbance, and economic collapse. But it was idleness that was frequently reported by travellers and politicians, many of whom tried unsuccessfully to disentangle the two and find some way of solving the intractable problems of Ireland. Some looked on this idleness harshly and scornfully, as is particularly shown by the quotation below, others in despair that these poor people wouldn't help themselves.

Both landlords and tenants are unfit for energetic exertion. The peasant's life is passed in planting potatoes in the spring, digging them up in the autumn and dozing through the winter over the turf fire that costs him nothing. The instant a misfortune falls upon him he is destitute and helpless. Improvident, ignorant and thriftless parents, scarcely human in habits and intelligence, present themselves with nine or ten skeleton children when they themselves can no longer support the pangs of hunger and their children are beyond recovery.

(Captain Kennedy reporting to the House of Commons in 1846)

The following comment is typical of many such directories in England and elsewhere but is hardly sympathetic to the plight of the poor of Galway:

'The climate (of County Galway), though subject to storms and rain, is peculiarly healthful; the prevalence of disease being more attributable to the habits of the humbler classes than to the influence of the atmosphere.'

(A Topographical Dictionary of Ireland, Samuel Lewis, 1837)

Poverty was often considered to be the just reward for idleness, and with a little effort and hard work even the idle Irish peasant could improve his standard of living himself without help from others who were enjoying the rewards of using well their God-given talents. There were plenty of examples of the idleness of Irish peasants who were thus blamed for their lot with little recognition of factors beyond their control that may have led to this situation.

This situation didn't only affect the agricultural base of Ireland. To complete the picture of Patrick's surroundings I should add that mineral deposits, coal, and iron that mainly lay along the banks of the mighty River Shannon and its tributaries were underdeveloped. Despite it being one of the major navigable rivers in Europe, the Shannon was almost completely undeveloped, whereas nearly every stream in Yorkshire had a mill or foundry on it using the power of the rushing water.

Round the city of Galway the fishermen were too disorganized to take advantage of the abundant harvest the Atlantic offered them and couldn't afford suitable boats or the salt to preserve their catches. Even during the famine years, when fish beyond the number to feed the fishermen could have saved the lives of others, there are no reports of this extra food being brought in from the sea. Who would have organised them to do such a thing?

A steam engine installed in a paper works in the city of Galway in about 1836 could have been the only piece of modern industrial equipment in the west of Ireland. In 1837 a large marble polishing machine was installed in the city but was powered by a treadmill in the county jail. The industrial revolution, in full progress in England at this time, hardly touched the west of Ireland.

There were exceptions of course. Carlo Bianconi built up his national network of coaches and inns from scratch. He foresaw the decline of coaches as railways grew, and as he ran down his coach empire he invested money in railways and became an extremely wealthy man. He was an Italian Catholic exile so perhaps nobody told him the history of Ireland and he had no preconceived ideas about the lowly status of Catholics in his adopted land. The canals were developed by Irish entrepreneurs as were the railways from the 1830s onwards but these were financed by Protestant businessmen and that's where the profits went too.

There were two Irelands that had arisen for legal, political, and economic reasons, which were now so ingrained and intertwined that ensuing problems seemed impossible to resolve. But the reasons for the lack of greater action must include the prevailing philosophies of the time. My purpose in telling this story of our Lally family is not only to illustrate how they lived, how they spoke, what they wore and ate, and how they travelled but how our ancestors and their fellows thought. How people thought is perhaps the most difficult thing for us to understand in the twenty-first century but we must judge people and events in the early nineteenth century on contemporary thinking and on what was acceptable then and not confuse this with modern twenty first century ideas.

In the early nineteenth century, people throughout Britain were much more familiar with death than they are today. Among children, neighbours, and family it was a frequent occurrence. Death of a breadwinner often led to the family being split up as happened to the family of Mary Lucy Lally, one of Patrick's daughters. She died in 1898 in London at the age of forty two, and her husband died eighteen months later. The six youngest of their nine children were split up into orphanages in Kent, Surrey, and Lancashire. The world was a cruel place, and tragedy was accepted as normal then. This may seem hard today, but if all these children's aunts and uncles and their older brothers were living in poverty how could they take on all these extra mouths?

Despite people being generally left to their own devices, the state could take control in ways that were cruel even then but were seen as normal. In the town where I now live, in 1847, Charles Groves, aged nine, was transported for seven years for stealing half a crown (12p) from a grocer in the High Street. He left behind his mother and father, brothers, sisters, and friends. Such occurrences were accepted. This is how people thought and how things worked, and you cannot judge our story of 200 years ago by current values.

As we shall see later, young Lally girls were sent from Loughrea to Australia in the 1840s. This did not only happen to the Irish. In 1836-37 there was a scheme under which girls and boys from workhouses in Hertfordshire were sent, by canal, to Manchester where there was work in the mills. In the 1840s and 1850s children from London workhouses were sent to work in the silk mill near where I write because the mill owners could not get workers locally because the work was hard and poorly paid. These children were probably sent for their own good—to find them work and a livelihood—and it was the duty of a workhouse master to minimise the burden on the Poor Rate. Such is the background to Patrick Lally's decision to move to England. When times were tough you had to pick yourself up and go where there was work. The alternative was the indignity and loss of freedom in the workhouse—or starvation.

Another widespread way of thinking at this time can be found in the highly influential writings of Rev. Thomas Malthus between 1798 and 1826. His philosophy stated that the growth of population will always be greater than the growth of food supply and this will be kept in balance by natural and inevitable checks to population growth such as war or starvation. Because population always grows ahead of the growth of food supply there are always poor people who die out due to their poverty or, in extreme cases, due to starvation. In the unchanging world, populations of humans and animals are naturally kept in check. The theory of Malthus was prominent and relevant enough to spur Parliament into assessing the size of the British population and to instigate the census held every ten years from 1801 building up to the first full and generally accurate census of 1841.

It was widely held that the world was unchanging. Continents, the weather, hills, mountains, and rivers had remained unchanged from their creation to the end of time. This divine providence also placed people in fixed positions in life. Before Darwin published his *Origin of Species* in 1859 it was thought that mankind was fixed and unchanged too. The theory that man could have developed from apes would have been ridiculed, as was the idea that strange shapes found in rocks had once been living dinosaurs. Antagonism to such notions as universal education and the building of railways was often based on this idea that such things presented the lower classes with ideas of a better way of life, would make them discontent with their lot and destabilise society. If workers went off looking for better things, the whole fabric of society would collapse. This, of course, proved to be true and resulted in the changes in society throughout the twentieth century.

According to prevailing social theory, one shouldn't meddle with the unalterable structure of nature and society. A good example of this thinking that divine providence fixed every man's place in society is in the words of a children's hymn still popular today. 'All Things Bright and Beautiful' was written in 1848, in the middle of the devastating Irish famine of which we will soon learn. It was written by Mrs Cecil F. Alexander, born in County Waterford, who married an Anglican priest who later became the Church of Ireland Bishop of Derry and then Archbishop of Armagh. It is a factual statement of the permanence of God's world.

First verse and Refrain
All things bright and beautiful
All creatures great and small
All things wise and wonderful
The Lord God made them all

Original third verse
The rich man in his castle
The poor man at his gate
God made them high and lowly
And ordered their estate.

One may think that, even by the standards of 1848, this third verse may have been considered tasteless just as over a million people were dying of starvation on her Irish doorstep. But this was not so. This verse is omitted from modern hymn books because it represents a philosophy no longer accepted but this was a popular hymn, sung in churches and schools all over the Empire by rich men and poor men alike until recent times. This would have been considered a statement of fact.

An event that showed another clear example of how people thought in the early nineteenth century occurred in 1834, right in the middle of this period we are studying. The Abolition of Slavery Act ended slavery in most of the British Empire. This campaign had been hard fought for many years and more than 5,000 British people who owned slaves, a wide and varied tranche of the upper classes from lords to businessmen and bishops, were compensated for the loss of their property. As well as the financial implications of abolition, it was considered by many that it was the lot of these people to be slaves, just as it was the lot of Irish Catholics to be kept in their place. Britain was generally a society of free men whose trade and social activity were generally unfettered by parliamentary interference but public opinion was changing. Under this pressure of public opinion parliament passed a number of pieces of legislation relaxing the restrictions placed on Catholics, culminating in The Catholic Emancipation Act of 1829. This act allowed Catholics to hold public office and to sit in parliament. The issues of slavery and Catholic emancipation demonstrated that the British public was beginning to accept that those groups that were positively discriminated against by legislation should be freed from this discrimination.

Ireland was used by the authorities as a classic example of all these philosophies and, as such, to try to solve these problems by human means was considered a waste of time. The Catholic Irish should be content with their lot, and largely, they were. Life for them wasn't fair or unfair. Life was life, controlled by God, the seasons, the weather, and harvest, and man couldn't alter any of those. The Irish poor, our Lallys included, would have seen themselves as a tiny part of a grand scheme, not its masters as many believe they are today. You played the hand you were given, but the rules of the game were set.

There are still adherents of these theories in the twenty-first century. In many parts of the world there are still strict and dramatic social divisions based on caste, sect, or tribe, so it should not be considered strange that they were widespread in Britain 200 years ago. We see today the same starvation in Africa and Asia to the extent that we get bored by the recurrence of appeals to feed these people and wonder why they can't sort their lives out themselves and use their natural resources of farmland and minerals. Today we could fly to Africa in a day or see the scenes of starvation in colour on our TVs and yet do little. To get to remote Loughrea from London would have taken a week, even after the railway linking London and Liverpool was completed in 1846.

6. Attempts at Solutions to Irish Problems

Many wealthy people considered it their duty to support the poor as the establishment of churches, schools, and hospitals testifies. In the early 1800s it certainly was not considered a duty of the state to get involved in people's lives in this way. But there were many who, regardless of philosophies and out of sheer compassion for the state of the Irish poor, fought for them personally, and thousands donated money to the first national charitable relief campaigns, which were run for the Irish poor. In Parliament there were now the first attempts to achieve something to alleviate their position.

Many political factors creating poverty in Ireland were common to other parts of Britain and Europe and cannot be considered to have been uniquely imposed upon the Irish by the English. Catholics were persecuted in England, perhaps not as much as in Ireland, but Catholics in England were such a small minority that it wasn't as conspicuous and they managed to get by better. The laissez faire policies of the British government, which left every man to fend for himself, were equally applied in all four countries of the United Kingdom.

The system of tithes, which so many Irish Catholic families, such as our own, paid to the established, Protestant church, also operated in England with a different effect. Tithes were grossly unfair in Ireland because the generally poor Catholics had to pay the generally richer Protestants who were the minority. This difference was not fully appreciated at the time. Education based on and promoting the Protestant faith was common throughout Britain, but in Ireland it disrupted the education of the majority and was seen as a key element of suppression and division. In Ireland it was the majority who suffered while the small minority of Catholics in England made their own arrangements and nobody noticed. In England there was some mobility of labour, as inadequate as it may be considered today, and workers could change employers or move to another place to find work. In England there was nothing to stop somebody moving up a notch or two in the class system, and this led to many of the great inventors and entrepreneurs of the nineteenth century coming from humble backgrounds. This was a key factor in England being the birthplace of the Industrial Revolution. None of this was the case in Ireland where there were rigid social and legal barriers to working men, mainly Catholics, preventing them from raising their status. There were few employers in Ireland, where most men rented a piece of land, so how could men change their job to better themselves. Ireland was very different, and the rulers in London didn't understand this, even if they claimed to be Irish lords. And the rulers of Ireland were a separate class, Protestant invaders, a class that Catholics could not join, who still ruled and punished the nation they defeated over 100 years earlier. The Irish could not rule themselves, and could not over the years solve their own problems so these problems became unsolvable.

Between The Act of Union in 1801 and 1845 there were 114 Commissions and 61 Special Committees set up by the British Parliament to look into the problems of Ireland, such was the awareness of the size of the problem. Ireland received a disproportionate amount of Parliamentary time but every move was argued against vigorously by both sides of the House and both sides of the Irish people. Catholics, 95 per cent of the Irish population, had no direct representation in their British Parliament. It was the Protestant Irish lords and landowners who claimed to be putting the views of their tenants to the House of Commons, but these contradicted the real views of the Irish tenants put forward in petitions and leaflets. Many of these petitions were not read out in the Houses of Parliament because the facts they revealed were too ghastly and appalling for the Members' ears.

THE MODERN SISYPHUS.

UNION IS STRENGTH.

John Bull.— "HERE ARE A FEW THINGS TO GO ON WITH, BROTHER, AND I'LL SOON PUT YOU IN A WAY TO EARN YOUR OWN LIVING."

THE ENGLISH LABOURER'S BURDEN;
OR, THE IRISH OLD MAN OF THE MOUNTAIN.

[See *Sinbad the Sailor*.

Punch cartoons that satirised the Irish situation.

"The Modern Sisyphus", 1844. In Greek mythology Sisyphus was doomed to eternally push an immense boulder up a hill, for it always to slip down to the bottom again just as he reached the top.
Here Robert Peel, the British Prime Minister, is shown as Sisyphus eternally rolling the Irish problem up the hill.

" Union is Strength – Here are a few things to go on with Brother, and I'll soon put you in a way to earn your own living", 1846. John Bull is giving a basket of bread and a shovel to Irish peasants.

"The English Labourer's Burden", 1849. The Irishman on the back of an English labourer is carrying a sack marked '£50,000', the amount of additional aid just given to Ireland by Britain.

The Marquis of Clanricarde made the point that it was widely felt by Irish Members and lords that the House shut its ears to discussion of Irish matters. He quoted an 'Honourable Friend' as saying,

> 'I have been many years a Member of the British House of Commons, and I have found that on all questions, except those relating to Ireland, I am listened to with attention; but I have often felt that the very fact of my being an Irish Member, lessens my influence on Irish subjects.' (Hansard, 26 June 1845, Vol.81, p.11970)

Surely the reason for this was that, despite many MPs and peers realising the enormity of the Irish problem, the very people they should turn to for advice, the Irish, could never agree among themselves and proposed solutions which were diametrically opposed and contradictory. The whole problem was intractable.

The 1838 Irish Poor Relief Act brought Ireland in line with the similar act passed for England in 1834, which had set up the new workhouses. It was forced through Parliament despite opposition, as usual, from all sides of Irish opinion. The arguments against the act were many, based on the many reasons why the English system would not work in Ireland. Firstly, the purpose of the English workhouse was, in addition to some provision for the sick, to force the idle and unfortunate to carry out useful work that would, in part, pay for their keep and encourage them to leave to better themselves in the greater world. This is why they were called 'work' houses. But the opposite would result in Ireland as the fear was that Irish workhouses would be filled with the able-bodied who wanted work that didn't exist.

It was also claimed that, whereas the English workhouse would be a place to be feared and avoided, it would be impossible to create an environment worse than normal Irish living conditions that might encourage inmates to leave. As the level of Poor Rate was to be based on local population it would greatly encourage evictions, particularly if landlords' consciences were partly relieved by the fact that those evicted had somewhere to go—the workhouse. The workhouses would be overwhelmed. All this would prove to be true, but there was a desperation in the British Parliament that something had to be done for Ireland. Resistance also came from English taxpayers who were to pay 50 per cent of the cost and who objected to constantly subsidising the Irish and also from Irish taxpayers, the Protestant landlords, who couldn't and wouldn't pay for what they saw as a blank cheque made out to the idle Catholic poor.

Alexander Somerville describes well how the Irish Poor Law worked in neighbouring Mayo, to the advantage, in this case, of Lord Lucan and to the disadvantage of the Catholic poor. His example is based on Castlebar, sixty miles north of Loughrea. This was a particularly bad case but he chose it to demonstrate the widespread abuses of the system. It is included in our story as an example of the environment that affected the lives of our family and goes some way to, again, explain the demoralisation of the Irish poor.

Lord Lucan was the major landowner in County Mayo. He was lord lieutenant of County Mayo. He was also head magistrate at Castlebar and chairman of the Poor Law Board of Guardians. His steward, the man responsible for management of the Lucan estates including collection of rents, evictions, etc., was principal acting magistrate and treasurer of the Poor Law Board of Guardians. The five workhouses built in County Mayo were on sites chosen by Lord Lucan, all within a few miles of each other while other parts of the county had no workhouse in forty miles. The sites enabled the landlords to sell poor land at a good price and have substantial buildings erected, all with cash advanced by the English Parliament. When the Poor

Law system collapsed, as they considered it surely would, the buildings could revert cheaply to the previous owners of the land. These workhouses were built by the local landlords who supplied the stones, sand, lime, timber, and labour, probably at full market prices.

With work, the labourers could now pay their rents and, in many cases, catch up with arrears to their landlords. The landlords were enabled, under the act, to pass on their 50 per cent share of the Poor Rate as increased rents to their tenants, which, of course, they could not pay. So the magistrate could send out police and army, both paid for by England, to evict the tenants for non-payment of rent. But Lord Lucan was the chief defaulter of the Poor Law Rate. He paid none of it. Yet no magistrate sent police or army to his handsome demesne, The Lawn, just outside Castlebar, across town from the new workhouse, because Lord Lucan was head magistrate.

The Loughrea Poor Law Union was set up on 5 September 1839. A new workhouse was built a mile south of the town on the banks of Lough Rea, which you may think could have been an attractive spot but, in fact, the 'gray lake' is bleak and windswept most of the time and was blocked from view by the 7 foot (2.1m) high walls enclosing the workhouse. It received its first inmate on 26 February 1842. The Loughrea

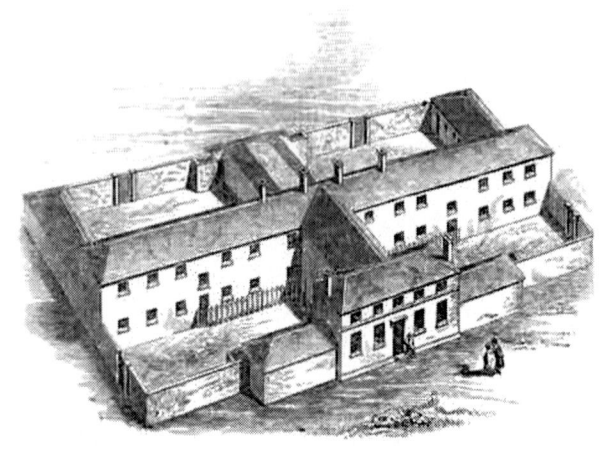

One of the standard plans for British workhouses.

Union covered an area of 197 square miles and included parishes stretching from Athenry, half way to Galway to the west, to Portumna on the banks of the Shannon 18 miles to the southeast, with Loughrea in the centre. The official population of the Union area in 1841 was 62,000 people. The new workhouse was a substantial building based on the standard design for 800 inmates and was built just in time. The impending crisis would see the population of Ireland fall by about 25 per cent between 1841 and 1851. The population of the Loughrea area was to fall by a third.

We have seen how, despite its almost total dependence on the potato and the fractured political and social structure of society, the Irish population had grown tremendously in a short time to the point at which it was unsupportable in all but the most favourable circumstances. These favourable circumstances were about to come to an end in the Great Famine of 1845 to 1849, which turned poverty into mass starvation on an unbelievable scale.

Was it possible to have done more than is detailed in this short chapter? Are the reasons described earlier really excuses? Is more done today for Africa where millions die in the same way? There had been many famines besides those in Ireland and their scale was such that organised, large-scale assistance was considered impossible and deaths were inevitable. The mind-set was that famines were a cruel twist of providence.

A quarter of the population of Iceland died after a volcanic eruption in 1783, and this, combined with the effects of El Niño, caused cold weather, which resulted in the death from starvation of many people across Europe over the following five years. For many 1816 was known as 'The Year Without Summer' when hundreds of thousands died of starvation across Europe and North America. This was probably caused by an historic low in solar activity and the enormous volcanic eruption of Mount Tabora in Indonesia. The potato blight of the 1840s caused great hardship and starvation in many parts of Europe, including Scotland.

The reaction of the British Government and people around the world to the Irish famine was unprecedented, and, despite the failure of their efforts, was the first major attempt at mass famine relief. The bad reputation of the English is not only because of their handling of the famine itself and the actions of some landlords, but the fact that they had overseen systems of the previous centuries that are seen to have played a large part in bringing the whole situation about and these grievances continued for another seventy years. Many writers, even 160 years after the Great Famine, are still vitriolic in their hatred of the English, and this attitude is good for business in some famine museums that are a feature of the modern Irish tourist industry. However, most textbooks try to give a more balanced view of the causes and the relief effort, and so have I. Even so, you cannot underestimate the misery of these times, and I'm afraid there is more to come as we look at the worst years of the Great Famine.

7. The Great Famine

Hail, Hail, Holy Queen, mother of mercy; hail our life, our sweetness and our hope. To thee do we cry, poor banished children of Eve. To thee do we send up our cries, mourning and weeping in this vale of tears. Turn then, most gracious advocate, thine eyes of mercy towards us. And after this, our exile, show unto us the blessed fruit of thy womb, Jesus. O clement, O loving, O sweet Virgin Mary. Pray for us, O holy Mother of God, that we may be made worthy of the promises of Christ. Amen.

(Conclusion to the recitation of the Holy Catholic Rosary)

Ireland had been wracked by famine many times since 1750. The poorest lived at the very bottom of existence, and even the landlords had no realisable capital, little cash, and often, a lot of debt. Their existence largely depended on the potato harvest, which was as fickle as the weather. Each year the size and quality of the crop was hidden underground and didn't reveal itself until it was dug in September or October.

On 25 July 1845 *The Times* in London reported the expectation of an excellent crop in Ireland. *The Times* frequently commented on the potato crop as it was growing in importance in the English working man's diet too, and unlike confidence in the dependability of other crops, the fear of a sudden realisation of failure could cause unrest among the working classes. But by August a new potato blight was being reported across Europe and in parts of southern England.

On 13 September 1845 the first outbreak of crop failure was reported from Ireland. By the beginning of October travellers were reporting that the lush, green, potato fields they had seen on travelling out from Dublin or Cork were, when they returned two days later, a sea of black rot. As digging commenced the full extent of the disaster became apparent. Even good news of healthy tubers being dug was soon replaced by stories of the stored potatoes decaying rapidly into a mess of putrid, black slime. In the Loughrea area this was reported in November. In just two months what had seemed an excellent crop had become a tragedy.

The ramifications of this for our Lally families and all the people of Ireland cannot be overestimated as everybody could see how they would be affected. Many were already hungry and in debt, as usual at this time of year, and they wrung their hands in horror as they looked at the destruction of their entire wealth for the coming year, at their inability to buy seed potatoes for the following year, and at almost certain eviction. Creditors could see no return of their loans; landlords would lose their rents and would not be able to pay their creditors. Taxes would not be paid. The Irish economy would stop and collapse, and that is what it did in the two years between November 1845 and 1848 when the full horror reached its peak.

The realisation of what must come was not lost on the British government. The following is the surviving first page of a letter from a Relief Commission inspector, which obtained wide distribution, including to the Lord Lieutenant of Galway and the British Government Minister.

Loughrea—7 March 1846 County of Galway

I regret very much to state that I have ascertained from personal inspection and particular enquiry from persons on whose credibility I can rely that potatoes in every direction for at least ten miles around this town are rotting at a most fearful rate. Pits of potatoes, which six weeks ago were perfectly sound, are now, half of them in a state of decomposition. The prospect is most horrifying—there are thousands of families in this neighbourhood (I mean a circle of two miles round) who will not have a single potato to subsist on against the middle of next May. There is no employment, I may say, at present in this locality, owing to the wetness of the season, and unless some public works are set on foot and means devised to keep down the prices of provisions which . . .

*Colonel McGregor, Inspector General,
Commission of Enquiry.*

Robert Peel, prime minister, was no friend of Ireland or the Irish, and he was a great supporter of the Corn Laws that restricted food imports and kept food prices high to benefit landowners. Yet he pushed for repeal of the Corn Laws to allow cheap imports in the full knowledge that it would bring down his government. He also took it upon himself to order £100,000 of Indian corn from the USA, bypassing lengthy parliamentary debate and procedures because he realised that quick action was needed for the Irish and to beat inevitable world price rises.

Over the following months a relief commission was set up to coordinate action in Ireland and with the promise to more than match any money raised by the British public. By 1846 relief works were under way, and up to 140,000 people were employed in this way at any one time. In total, in 1845-46, the British Government spent £365,000 and gave as much again in loans despite such action being totally against their laissez-faire principles.

Alongside this unparalleled official relief effort there was the largest-ever public charitable campaign, run by the churches and by local groups that sprang up on reading news of the constant parliamentary debate and of the plight of their Irish neighbours in all the English newspapers, many of which sent reporters to bring back details. Donations of £100 and £50 were not uncommon, and towns such as Bridgewater, Somerset with a population of 10,000 raised £1,100 in a few weeks. Enormous fundraising took place among the Irish in

America, and the British Government agreed to pay the cost of shipping any free goods to Ireland from there. Donations poured in from all over the Empire.

All these good intentions and expenditure must have had some effect, but in terms of preventing disaster they failed. In Ireland there was no way of implementing the actions that could have turned the situation around. There was no infrastructure, skills, or experience on which to base these charitable activities, and efforts to do good were overwhelmed by the sheer numbers of people and the extent of the crisis.

To start with, the purchase of Indian corn proved to be impractical. During the journey from America it had sweated and overheated and was as hard as flint. It could not be ground using conventional millstones and in Ireland not even conventional mills existed in sufficient quantity to grind this vast amount of corn. The Irish ate potatoes that didn't need mills. It proved impossible to tranship this corn around the country by road. By sea there were not enough suitable small ships to get into the small and undeveloped harbours of the west coast where the grain was most needed.

The British Government's thinking was that relief should be handled by normal tradesmen. It was not the job of government to bypass them in any way. If food, for example, was provided direct to the poor or to workhouses, the government would destroy the businesses of wholesalers and retailers as so often happens in African famine areas today. What they failed to appreciate was that such trading structures hardly existed in Ireland, particularly in the west of Ireland. As previously mentioned, few people risked capital for a potential profit. Inevitably huge blockages appeared in the supply chains, particularly in ports, as no adequate system existed to further distribute it. There were so very few wholesalers or retailers or hauliers.

Similarly, relief works were impeded by a lack of skilled managers and of those who could be trusted with the expenditures and cash for wages. No skilled surveyors, quantity surveyors, or assessors of piece work existed. Although some successful schemes were undertaken, many roads were built that went nowhere, walls that were built for no apparent reason and that were never used. Many landlords demanded high prices for the land to build new roads, and there was nobody who could or who dared to negotiate with them. Some landlords took the opportunity to rebuild roads past their own front doors. Construction works made roads impassable for weeks while nothing happened due to bad management, lack of materials, or bad weather.

Armed Irish peasants wait for a meal cart.

This threat meant that meal carts went out under military escort.

The relief convoys couldn't get out from the main ports in the east to the west of Ireland where food supplies were most needed. Slow-moving convoys were attacked by starving locals as they trundled past, so the military was brought in to guard them. Sometimes there was no food to buy with the wages earned on government schemes, and while men were working in this way, they were not planting next year's crops, so the famine was being extended. Some innovative schemes were proposed that would have long-term benefits, such as the public improvement of farmland to enable the future planting of a wider variety of crops in greater quantity. But these all failed due to arguments over whose land should be improved and the general refusal of landowners to pay even the half of the cost they were asked for. There were very few successful schemes but one was just a few miles from Loughrea. For a hundred years attempts had been made to make the River Shannon navigable by large boats for almost its entire length. In 1846 the Government Board of Works took over the duties of the Shannon Commissioners and installed improved canals and locks for 115 miles north of Portumna.

Somehow most people survived the winter of 1845-46 on the few potatoes that were not blighted and on other crops they had planted or by killing the pig or chicken and on handouts. By the spring of 1846 they had nothing to eat or to plant but struggled on during the summer on a diet of wild berries and edible roots and on cabbage leaves. Time and again they would scrabble through the potato field to see if there was one more potato they had missed.

A boy and girl searching for that missed potato

Many who could afford the fare left, much against their Irish instinct to stay with family and friends. They were demoralised and already nearly starving so for most of them who had never travelled further than a day's journey the fear of how they would survive with no money or contacts in a foreign land kept them at home. Groups of starving men roamed the country begging for food and trying to intimidate others not to pay rents and to threaten landlords who didn't pay their share of the relief funds. The Earl of Clanricarde, safe in London, presented a Bill for the Protection of Life in Ireland to parliament which proposed what amounted to marshal law and the great reinforcement of troops to enforce it.

With the failure of the small crop in October 1846 and with the early onset of winter in November, panic began to set in. The public-works schemes began to collapse because they were overrun by applicants, thousands of them. In County Galway there were three times the applicants that could be afforded or accommodated. Men and boys forced themselves onto the works insisting on being employed. Priests would march groups of parishioners to works demanding their right to work and be paid. The crowds meant that there was no room to work, and even in better organized groups little work was done because the men were too weak for manual labour. To avoid riots, with spades and pickaxes to hand, often all were paid until the money ran out after which not one was paid.

The winter weather of 1846-47 was the worst in living memory. Instead of warm winds blowing off the Atlantic, icy north winds covered the whole of northern Europe for months. Snow covered even the west of Ireland and parts of the Shannon froze over. The whole Irish society began to collapse. There was no work, no money, and very little food to buy even if you had money. Roads were impassable, and there were stories of horses sinking in to the mud up to their chests and nobody being able to dig them out. People lay on dung heaps to keep warm. A great fear of impending doom began to grip all levels of society.

The reaction of landlords to this disaster varied enormously. Lord Lucan, in neighbouring County Mayo, saw only one solution for the troubles of Ireland: a large part of the population must disappear and he cared not where. It was Lord Lucan and his type who earned for the English the hatred of the Irish which has passed down through the centuries. His tenants who had not paid their due rent were evicted in tens of thousands, and anybody who sheltered them was evicted too. He was known throughout Connaught as 'The Great Exterminator'. His contribution to Ireland was the invention of an infernal machine that, by a system of wooden beams and levers, could, with one crack of a whip and a pull of the horses, demolish a house. He boasted that two of these machines enabled a sheriff to evict as many families in a day as a team of fifty men with crowbars—his 'Crowbar Brigades'. Whole villages were razed in this way. When attacked in the House of Commons he accused his attackers' desire to waste money on useless paupers as criminal sentimentality. It was Lord Lucan who allowed his local workhouse in Castlebar, which had never had more than 140 inmates despite being built to house 800, to go bankrupt when he was the major creditor because he refused to pay his Poor Rate. This was in October 1846 before the worst had come.

On the other hand, the Earl of Sligo in the north of Connaught, brought himself to the brink of bankruptcy by his active relief works. Twice his donations had personally prevented the bankruptcy of Westport workhouse. At the age of 28 he kept no staff and had not even a carriage. In the end, being responsible by law for the taxes of his tenants in holdings worth under £4, the majority, he either evicted or would be declared bankrupt and be evicted himself. For the sake of his family heritage he had to hold on to his estates in the hope of starting again.

So who was more right or wrong—Lucan, who cruelly evicted at the start and then could improve the efficiency of his land, or Sligo, who compassionately hung on till the point of bankruptcy before evicting and then had no money to improve his land? It is the likes of Lucan who are remembered, but there were many like Sligo who are forgotten because their meagre resources didn't have much effect against the tidal wave of the tragedy and their bankruptcies meant that they too disappeared from history.

And what part did Clanricarde, the largest landowner in the west of Ireland and principal landowner in and around Loughrea, play in this tragedy? He was probably the landlord who would most directly have affected the lives of Patrick and his family. He entered the British cabinet as Postmaster General in 1846 just as the Great Famine was beginning.

Clanricarde's actions typified so many of those involved in Ireland at the time, particularly politicians who had to act on their words and ideas, not just propound them. His actions and ideas were contradictory and he often changed his mind. He didn't seem to carry out his own government's policies on his own estates, despite seeing himself as the champion of Irish affairs in Parliament. I suspect that, like so many, he was floundering and failing to find solutions to the impossible problems of Ireland.

In 1848, at the height of the Great Famine and coinciding with the celebrations of his son's coming of age, many hovels in Loughrea were demolished and their occupants cast onto the streets. Can these have been the actions of his agent, D'Arcy, without Clanricarde's knowledge? It was suggested that they were. Clanricarde was responsible for promoting legislation in Parliament to support the destitute in Ireland but was accused of a lacklustre performance because he was keen to protect the landlords too. He supported or declined to criticise many local landlords who were accused of cruel evictions and many statements showed that he saw this as an essential part of land reform.

Clanricarde was prominent in the promotion of emigration and in 1839 offered to pay the passage and give £5 to any pauper tenant who emigrated. Yet when, after the Great Famine, Ireland was denuded he complained that it was the most capable and enterprising who left:

> 'The US will have gained enormous wealth and resources by the Irish famine and the Irish Poor Law. All who should have tilled or should be tilling Irish soil in Mayo and Galway, which is left untilled, have been carried off to clear land in America.'

During the Great Famine it is clear that Clanricarde accepted as inevitable the fact that many would die so his efforts to save human life must have been limited by this belief. In Parliament he supported the extension of poor relief to those outside the workhouse yet stated that he would not cooperate with outside relief in Loughrea where he had enormous practical influence, even if no specific role. In February 1848 the Loughrea Board of Guardians was replaced because of their gross negligence in maintaining the service and collecting the Poor Rate and this in an area of land and tenants dominated by the holdings of Clanricarde.

Clanricarde is a demonstration of the complexity of the Irish problem: Protestant father, Catholic mother, Irish landowner, British government minister. His right hand often did the opposite of his left hand to juggle the system. He had seen much of his Irish estates sold off over generations to pay debts partly caused by the lack of viability of Irish agriculture. He probably supported land reform and the reduction of the population as the only pragmatic way of solving Ireland's problems and his own. If he accepted that many would die he would have to admit to himself that the cost in human life, though terrible, was a price worth paying—for those who survived.

And what example do we see set by the Daly family of Dunsandle who owned much land to the north of Loughrea, including at Kiltullagh? Among many other roles Lord Dunsandle was chairman of the Midland Great Western Railway Company, which was constructing the line from Dublin to Galway. He also proposed a government scheme to drain large areas of land. Both projects would not only provide a large amount of work but also, on completion, bring great economic benefits to the area. He said that this would be meaningful, useful, and rewarding work for the labouring class that had become too accustomed to the free handouts then being provided on the strength of the Poor Law Rates. The following report from the *Galway Vindicator* in March 1847 shows the actions of his second son, Skeffington, at the family house.

> *It has been communicated to us by a gentleman who happened to visit Dunsandle on Wednesday last that he never felt more gratified by witnessing the charitable labours of the Hon. Captain Skeffington Daly with the Hon Miss Daly in the distribution of Indian Meal, oatmeal and herrings to the numerous poor in the district at very reduced prices. The provision store is established in one of the out offices of the family mansion and the stock purchased at their own private expense.*

Lord Dunsandle was chairman of the Loughrea Board of Guardians but in August 1847 he and another member of the Board died of fever contracted at the workhouse. His son, Denis St George, inherited the title unexpectedly early and, with it, a place on the Board of Guardians. He may have set the tone at his very first meeting by proposing the postponement of the appointment of Relieving Officers, the men who would have administered outdoor relief. The management of the Loughrea Workhouse deteriorated to the point that the whole Board was dismissed by the Irish Poor Law Commissioners in February 1848 for refusing to administer outdoor relief and for the dreadful conditions there. The workhouse was run until November by a board imposed by the commissioners but the chairman of the new board from November 1848 was the new Lord Dunsandle, presumably now reluctantly prepared to follow the rules.

Perhaps we can judge the attitude and actions of the new young lord at the workhouse by what we know of his running of his estates. Whatever the evils of the old Lord Dunsandle, the new lord was even worse and immediately exhibited an aggressive attitude to the problems of his tenants by evicting many of them to make farms of an economic size. He became known as The Lord Leveller in July 1848 when forty cabins were demolished in just one day. He didn't see these poor people as his responsibility. They were squatters standing in the way of the development of economic agriculture.

But there was an influence over him that led to a marked softening of his views towards his Catholic tenants. Denis St George was a notorious womaniser renowned for relationships with woman well below his class and as early as 1835 had built a so-called hunting lodge, Attymon House, in which to hide his liaisons. While activity against his Catholic tenants was going on in 1847-48 he set up house at Attymon for Mary Broderick, a tenant farmer's daughter who was to bear him many children before he eventually married her in 1864 on threat of eternal damnation from her Catholic parish priest.

Not much else stood in his way. He even built a new road so that he didn't have to pass the new Catholic Chapel in Kiltullagh when he was travelling between Dunsandle and Attymon

House to visit his mistress. Was this due to his respect for God or because the Catholic priest leapt out and berated him whenever he drove past? Mary is credited with many good works, presumably with Dunsandle money, with interceding on behalf of tenants, and with softening the attitude of Denis towards them. I include this story because his many sides: an arch-Tory capitalist, aggressive Protestant landowner with a Catholic peasant mistress illustrates so well the complexity of Ireland.

Our Lally family, whether or not they were still Dunsandle tenants, would have known all this. What did a good Catholic family, if good is what they were, think of all this?

The Illustrated London News reported in December 1849 that a total of 254,000 holdings of between one and five acres and the houses on them had been destroyed between 1841 and 1848. These were the livelihoods and homes of 60 per cent of the lowest class. There were good economic reasons for this—they were just not viable—but it is impossible just to read of evictions and pass on without thinking of the ramifications. That word 'eviction' brought terror to the hearts of the peasants. Here is a part of a report from *The Tablet* of July 1848 concerning the area in which our Lallys lived.

> *I never felt so appalled by human suffering and so incensed against the cruelty of landlords as when witnessing the exterminating system which is now being carried out between Attymon and Kiltullagh by Lord Dunsandle . . .*
>
> *. . . We were attracted by the smoke that rose from the sooty ruins of a peasant's cabin which Lord Dunsandle and the Sherriff had previously demolished. Suspecting that some unfortunate creatures whose dwelling had been torn down still lingered among the ruin we went to examine and found*

that our suspicions were just for under one of the walls we found a sort of temporary shed made of a few stones loosely thrown upon each other and covered with green turf.

A poor, emaciated, half naked, sallow-complexioned female of middle age made her appearance at the door of the miserable smoky hovel for it had no chimney but the door. We asked her some questions while we felt horror stricken at finding any of our fellow creatures reduced to such indescribable wretchedness. Her doleful story of double ruin may be told in a few words. She had spent the greater part of her life in that house—her children were born in it and she clung in desperation to the ruins when the roof was torn off and the walls torn down under the inspection and direction of Lord Denis Daly and the sheriff of the county. She said that she had owed ten shillings!!

. . . Between Esker and Kiltullagh the number of demolished cabins is frightful. When at the pretty little church of Kiltullagh, recently built by public subscription, a half famished female . . . told us that the church was now become almost useless for all the people who contributed to its erection were gone. We asked wither—to America? She with a sigh answered, "Alas, Sir, not quite so far; that would be too expensive to Lord Dunsandle. They are gone to Kilnadrish (a churchyard a short distance off) where some of them went even without a coffin for they starved and died when driven out of their cabins by this Lord."

I have heard from good authority that this Lord Denis, of exterminating celebrity, had the cruelty to say that the population of Ireland is yet twice too numerous.

The English press was full of stories of the horrors in Ireland. Here Alexander Somerville comes down firmly against Irish nobility and Irish landlords in one of his 1847 letters for *The Manchester Examiner:*

> *When we bring to mind that Ireland does not pay the assessed taxes, nor several of the other excise duties, (that on soap, for instance) nor income nor property tax; that Irish landlords were never until now taxed for public roads and that they now unite into an 'Irish Party' to harass the government and impose upon the English new burthens for performance of duties which they neglect, it will be seen that, as a class, Irish landowners stand at the bottom of the scale of honest and honourable men.*

As he travelled in Ireland for the newspaper he wrote this from Banagher, about twenty-five miles east of Loughrea.

A starving widow and her children

> *At the place where I write a father, mother and two children came into the street at night and lay down on the pavement. They came from the neighbouring town, they said, because they could get no food there. At about 8 o'clock the woman went to the door of the house adjoining and begged for a piece of turf to make a fire in the street for her husband was dying. It happened to be the temporary lodgings of a naval officer of Her Majesty's service and it need hardly be said that the request was at once complied with and more than turf given. At 10 o'clock the woman called at the door again begging for a piece more turf, for that her husband was dead and they*

were lying beside the cold body. The Officer went out and found this to be the case. He proceeded to the constabulary station but the constables would do nothing with the dead body, nor the survivors who lay beside it, till morning. He proceeded elsewhere and procured some straw for them and made a bed and got stakes and put a shelter over their heads and made and administered a warm meal for them. In the morning he was astir in time to relieve them and, going out, met some constables, the principal of whom talked loud and angrily to the woman for having her husband dead on that side of the street. "Just", said the honest English sailor to me in relating the case, "as if there should be etiquette observed in the dying of hunger." . . . I am willing to believe that the overwhelming amount of distress, rather than the people's natural feelings, makes them callous and hard hearted.

And this from Limerick when he was unable to pass through to Galway because of the driving and drifting snow:

To continue to tell of all the ghastly faces, hollow and shrunken, which I have seen, with death looking out of the eyes, might horrify and appal the reader but would, I fear, instruct him. The masses of the population amongst whom I have travelled . . . sinking from health to sickness, from life to death—not yet dead but more terrible to look upon and think upon than if they were dead; living but with death and his attendants in possession of the human tenement and keeping possession until the indwelling spirit of clay is ejected, thrown out, out at the windows where it is already to be seen struggling to stay within and glaring horribly upon the passer by; those masses of the population would afford, in description, scope enough to fill this paper from title to printer's name.

Josephine Butler was to become a prominent Christian campaigner for women's rights, the rights of prostitutes, abolition of slavery, and concern for the socially disadvantaged. She said that what she witnessed while staying in Ireland when she was nineteen in 1847 was a founding event in her beliefs and her campaigns in later life.

A widow and her dying child.

As a young girl I had no conception of the full meaning of the misery I saw around me, yet it printed itself upon my brain and memory. I can recollect being awakened in the early morning by a strange sound like the chattering of many birds. Some of the voices were hoarse and almost extinguished by the faintness of famine; and on looking out of my window I recollect seeing the garden and fields in front of the house completely darkened by a population of men, women and children, squatting in rags; uncovered skeleton limbs protruding everywhere from their wretched clothing and clamorous, though faint, voices uplifted for food . . . . I recollect too, when walking through the lanes and villages, the strange morbid famine smell in the air, the sign of approaching death even in those who were dragging out a wretched existence. Nor can I forget the occasional shrill wail which was sighed out by some poor creature sending out her last cry of despair to heaven before falling down in a state of collapse by the wayside.

Reports to the government covered the plagues of scurvy, typhus, relapsing fever, and 'the bloody flux', brought on by eating raw turnips, seaweed or half-cooked Indian meal. This added to the problems in workhouses and the few hospitals. People were filthy as well as starving; they ate unwashed food when they could and they huddled together under one blanket for warmth. All these factors led to fevers that spread from person to person through bodily contact. Whole towns fell to fever and visitors, thinking the town deserted but attracted by the stench, found the dead and just living huddled together, the living not having the strength or will to move.

Loughrea was not immune from this scourge, the following events being recorded in the press.

> *An inquest was held on view of the body of Catherine Daly of Knockbarron, near Loughrea, by Thomas Walsh Esq. and a respectable jury, when after the examination of several witnesses (one of whom was sister of the deceased) who deposed that the deceased had lived for some time past chiefly on turnips and, for taking some (turnips) while labouring under the pangs of hunger, she was committed to prison. After her discharge she had not wherewithal to support existence and died from starvation. The jury returned a verdict accordingly.*
>
> *(The Nation, 5 February 1848)*

> *An inquest was held by Thomas Walsh Esq. on the body of Thomas Fahy, aged 40 years, of Kilchreest, near Loughrea. One of the witnesses, Mr Saggerton, in whose house the inquest was held, deposed that deceased was brought to his house by one of the witnesses, Mr Hawkins. He was a complete skeleton, reduced to skin and bone and his appearance was frightful. Mr Hawkins stated that he found deceased lying in an exhausted state and carried him to the*

house of Mr Saggerton, did not suppose he could be more than three stone in weight, so reduced was he by starvation and want. The jury returned a verdict of "died from extreme want and destitution".

(The Nation, 5 February 1848)

PROGRESS OF ANNIHILATION—The destruction of human life has now become so regular that no amount of mortality is now regarded as extraordinary or excessive. The weekly average of deaths in the several unions (of County Galway) may afford a test of the gradual decline of the population and it will be a subject well worthy the investigation of political economists to ascertain how the destruction of animal life by the steady action of starvation leads, by the removal of the surplussage of population, to advance the prosperity of the country in which such a humane experiment is being tried. We learn that the number of individuals buried weekly from Loughrea workhouse exceeds fifty and we are informed that the Ballinasloe Workhouse is almost emptied by the active course of death in that bastille . . . . Hence we may fairly compute that, after the lapse of six months, the entire population will not exceed three and a half million.

(Galway Vindicator, reported in Freemans Journal, 21 April 1848)

Captain Hellard, an Englishman who had volunteered to oversee the fair distribution of British Association money in County Galway died of the fever he picked up in his inspections as did many others who volunteered to help. In the west of County Galway, which was almost totally depopulated by the end of 1847, two out of three doctors died in that one year. Such data is fragmentary but it is also recorded that at least seven doctors died between Galway and Loughrea. In the whole of Ireland there were only 28 hospitals and 450 dispensaries or clinics as we might call them, of which Loughrea had one, so the death rate of doctors in our area of interest must have been nearly as high as to the west.

It was the same with Catholic priests and nurses who tended the sick and reporters, charity workers, and other visitors who never returned from the plague-hit land. Deaths hit all classes, tenant and landlord, and all religions as the fever spread and as food became impossible, at times, to buy at any price. The following is a report from *The Illustrated London News* of 16 January 1847. One wonders why such an event was news but perhaps if this was reporting an event which took place in December it was not yet seen as an everyday event.

> *In a list of seven deaths specified in the Galway Mercury there is an account of the death of a man named Walker who, a few years ago, was the proprietor of a veterinary establishment in Dublin. It appears that on Thursday last he fell down suddenly in the town of Loughrea and, after a few minutes, expired. An inquest was held on the body and the jury returned a verdict of "Died of starvation."*

It is no wonder that records that may have helped the family historian today were never properly compiled. They would have originated from people suffering the same fate and who were overwhelmed by the tragedy surrounding them. The deaths were beyond counting and occurred not only in workhouses and hospitals but in homes, hedgerows, and ditches all over Ireland. The following is part of a letter to the *Galway Advertiser* on 27 February 1847. It not only points out how the people of Loughrea were suffering but also shows that the Marquis of Clanricarde was neglecting his duties by not appointing a seneschal, or mayor, and coroners who may have better controlled, recorded, and advertised what was happening.

At a time, says our correspondent, when death is decimating the ranks of our unfortunate poor and when every town and village and hamlet . . . has its records full to competition of death from starvation it may be thought that we of this town and vicinage are in comparative health and comfort and, to a certain extent, unscathed by the present destroying scourge, but such is not the case. The deaths here are unremitting and numerous but they pass unnoticed because their frequency has ceased to be wonderful. Had we one or more coroners in the district, he continues, the rest of our countrymen would at least perceive that we are suffering as much, if not more than, most other parts of the island.

The scene at the gate of a workhouse as desperate people wait to be allowed in.

As money ran out workhouses began to close. In January 1847 The British Association for the Relief of Extreme Distress in Ireland and Scotland was formed and quickly raised £435,000. This was to be distributed to those workhouses in most need, but Loughrea Workhouse did not qualify for this extra relief.

In 1849 twenty-two workhouses in the west of Ireland were declared bankrupt, but Loughrea Workhouse was not one of them. So the Loughrea Workhouse must have been better than most, yet, in early 1848, this was the situation described by a Poor Law inspector in Loughrea Workhouse, built to house 800. The inmates of Loughrea Workhouse almost certainly included some of Patrick's relatives and our ancestors, as we shall see.

> *I found 1,127 paupers, 12 of whom were in the idiot cells, 76 in the fever sheds, 58 in the infirmary, 60 in the male and female infirm dormitories . . . making a total of 206 on the sick list . . . The yard and privy at the female side were still more disgracefully dirty than at the male side. The sight was sufficient to sicken any person, the stench almost sure to do so . . . The nursery smoked so as to render it difficult to remain many minutes . . . yet it contained 36 women and 36 infants . . . we found deceased paupers deposited in shallow pits . . . In truth, the dead were lying in their graves within a few feet of the living.*

As we have seen, it was in August 1847 that Lord Dunsandle, chairman of the Loughrea Board of Guardians, and another Board member died of fever contracted at the workhouse. In the following February the Loughrea Board of Guardians was removed because of their refusal to administer outdoor relief and the appalling conditions in the workhouse itself. *The Nation* newspaper recorded the event on 26 February:—

> *The Loughrea Guardians are indignant at the manner in which they were dismissed by the Poor Law Commissioners. The affairs of the union were on the point of being satisfactorily arranged and the necessary steps taken to provide larger accommodation for the poor, when the order of dismissal*

arrived. No notice was given. The town of Loughrea, once very prosperous, is now almost one large lazar house*.

(*'lazar house'—house for poor, diseased, incurable persons—Oxford Dictionary.)

However the new vice-guardians accused the removed Board of Guardians of gross negligence:

The probation wards of the workhouse were in a most terrible state, wet, filthy and conducive to the spread of disease. A heap of dirty straw was piled up in one corner and several panes of glass were broken in the windows. The women in the day rooms crouched together in masses to keep each other warm. The water pumps were all out of order and the pipes broken or destroyed. Female paupers, almost in a state of nudity, carried the water required by the workhouse from the nearby lake. The Indian meal stirabout fed to the inmates was thin and burned, while the milk supplied to the workhouse was more than half water. Many paupers were served with sour porter or beer instead of milk to take with their porridge. The kitchen boilers were in a disgraceful state of rust while the floors of the dormitories were disfigured and rotting from urinal and other discharges. The workhouse sewers were out of order and the cesspools had not been completed. The place used as a burial ground was most unsuitable for that purpose as it adjoined the workhouse on a layer of hard rock so that graves could not be dug to a sufficient depth.

(From a chapter by John Joseph Conwell MA in The District of Loughrea, Vol.1)

The British Association inspector, Captain Hellard, who was mentioned earlier, wrote before his death of the diseases prevalent in County Galway workhouses:

> *The younger inmates of County Galway hospitals and workhouses are attacked in considerable numbers by a peculiar and fatal nervous disease. It is characterised by the most extreme stiffness of all the muscles, similar to that which occurs in lockjaw, and by such increased sensitiveness of the skin that the slightest touch or draught of air produces intense agony. It is induced by the preceding scarcity of food and is not communicable from one person to another.*

It is possible to look in detail at the activities of Loughrea Workhouse at this time because the minutes of the weekly meetings of the Board of Governors have survived. Several paupers by the name of Lally are mentioned, so, if for that reason alone, it is worth taking a look at what was going on there. The workhouse was by far the biggest operation in the area at the time, affecting every aspect of life in and around Loughrea. If we take one month, October 1848 when the Lally girls left for Australia, as an example, the population of the town of Loughrea was a little over 4,000, but the number of workhouse inmates rose above 2,000, peaking at 2,876 the following February.

Not only was there the main workhouse a little to the south of the town, but in that month the brewery and several houses in the town centre were taken over to increase the Workhouse capacity from 800 to 1,580, just as the actual number of inmates reached 2,000. In addition the workhouse administered outdoor relief to another 2,000, rising above 3,000 in the winter. The workhouse was a massive operation dominating the town.

There were not more than a dozen towns in the whole of County Galway with a larger population than just the actual inmates of Loughrea Workhouse. It was the biggest employer by far. The Minute Books mention the master, his assistants, matrons, medical officers and nurses, cooks, teachers, maintenance men, laundry staff, porters, buyers, and administrators. There were relief officers who managed and controlled the outdoor relief, which was a constant cause of concern as it was wide open to abuse.

While other workhouses were going bankrupt or refusing to take in more paupers than they could afford, from where did Loughrea get its money? Perhaps because the Loughrea Board of Guardians had been appointed by the Poor Law Commissioners earlier in 1848 they were more diligent in collecting the Poor Rates. They employed six collecting officers to travel the area collecting the Poor Rate from landowners (£2,664 in October) and late collecting officers who at the end of that month were chasing £4,929 overdue and instituting legal proceedings against defaulters.

Just look at the purchases of food alone in the four weeks of October, converted to modern metric measures.

10.9 tonnes of indian meal	20,000 litres of milk and buttermilk
6.9 tonnes of oatmeal	914 kilos of salt
4.3 tonnes of rice	221 kilos of sugar
4.0 tonnes of bread	132 kilos of meat
	82 kilos of cocoa and
	6 kilos of tea

It appears from the minutes that they may have grown their own potatoes.

Here was a major logistics operation, and carts must have been queuing all day to unload, along with those delivering hundreds of yards of calico and thread, wool, shoe nails, and old rope for oakum picking to keep the inmates busy, plus peat for fires, aprons, lantern oil, coffins, and so much more. This is a unique microcosm of a strange part of Loughrea life and it demonstrates that the economy had not completely collapsed. Food was available, and carts delivered it; big contracts were bid for and fulfilled. It shows that life and business, in part, continued even during these dreadful times. And buttermilk, cocoa, and meat? They were still available, and surely their presence in the orders shows budgets were not pinned down to save the last farthing.

While all these dreadful things were occurring the other Ireland still existed. On the marriage of the youngest son of Lord Dunsandle in January 1846, his uncle, the Church of Ireland Bishop of Cashel and Waterford 'bestowed upon his nephew the splendid gift of £80,000' (*Freemans Journal*). Splendid—I should say so! Is this the same Dunsandle family who tore down the hovels of their tenants while they were still inside? There was fashionable society in Dublin, and its activities continued while thousands of destitute emigrants poured through the city and queued at the soup kitchens every day. Society marriages, balls, achievements, and just their comings and goings were recorded in the regular 'Fashionable Intelligence' column in *Freeman's Journal*:

> *The Earl of Leitrim and suite, Rev Mr Caulfield, Mr & Mrs Adair and family, Messrs and Mrs Pakenham, Ponsonby, Plunkett, Calcraft, Cunningham . . . (etc, etc) . . . sailed from Kingstown for Liverpool on Thursday evening by her Majesty's mail packet (boat) Duke of Cambridge.*
>
> *(1 July 1848)*

Even in the height of the famine, paddle steamers were taking passengers on pleasure cruises from the same docks from which the starving masses were struggling to get a crammed passage to Liverpool.

PLEASURE TRIP
TO
BEAUMARIS AND BANGOR.

The Powerful   Steam Ship

" DUKE OF CAMBRIDGE,"

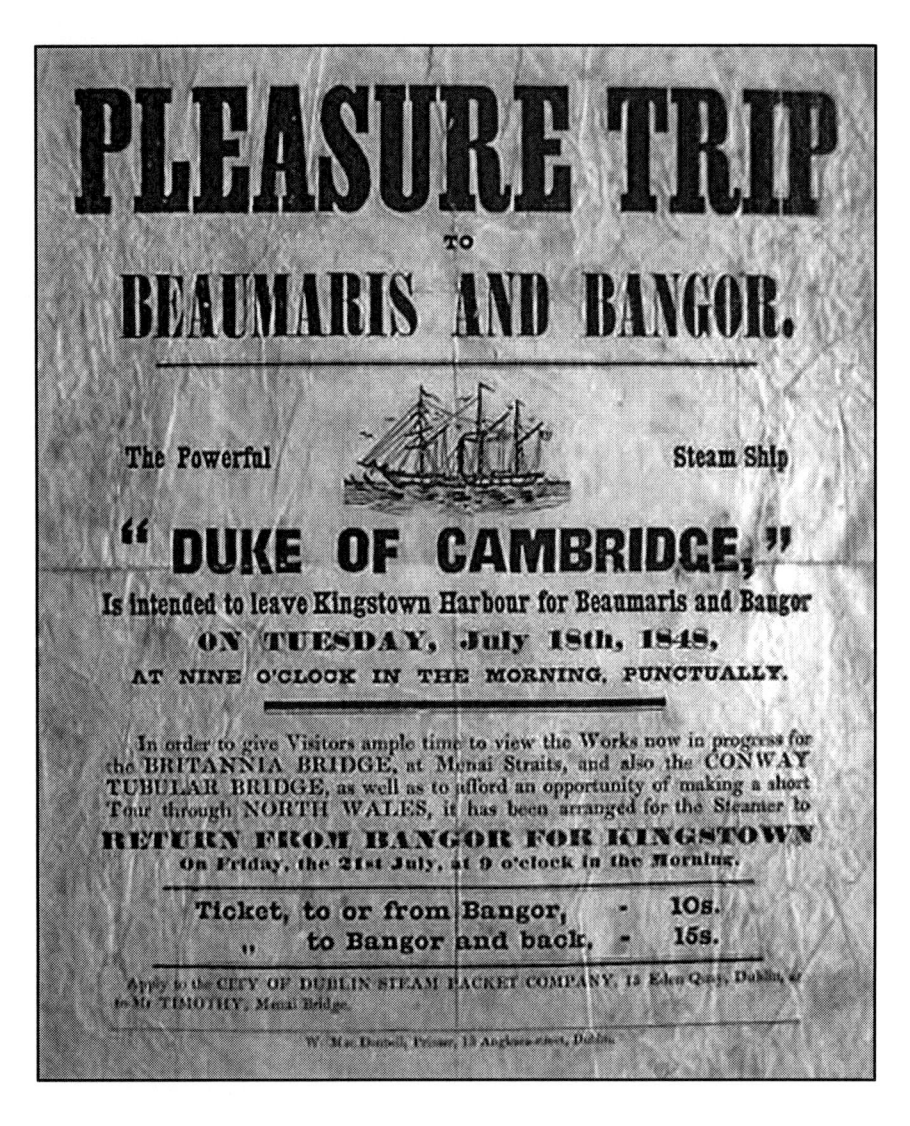

Is intended to leave Kingstown Harbour for Beaumaris and Bangor
ON TUESDAY, July 18th, 1848,
AT NINE O'CLOCK IN THE MORNING, PUNCTUALLY.

In order to give Visitors ample time to view the Works now in progress for the BRITANNIA BRIDGE, at Menai Straits, and also the CONWAY TUBULAR BRIDGE, as well as to afford an opportunity of making a short Tour through NORTH WALES, it has been arranged for the Steamer to
RETURN FROM BANGOR FOR KINGSTOWN
On Friday, the 21st July, at 9 o'clock in the Morning.

Ticket, to or from Bangor,	10s.
" to Bangor and back,	15s.

Apply to the CITY OF DUBLIN STEAM PACKET COMPANY, 15 Eden Quay, Dublin, or to Mr TIMOTHY, Menai Bridge.

W. MacDonnell, Printer, 13 Anglesea-street, Dublin.

By the middle of 1849 the worst of the disaster had passed, but all the Lally ancestors we are studying here had already left. Richard B Sheriden Esq. MP visited workhouses across Ireland to determine for himself the situation of which he had heard so much. He wrote the following note in the Loughrea Workhouse visitor's book:

I visited this house and inspected every portion of it. I was greatly struck by the extreme cleanliness and order throughout the establishment. The ventilation appeared most satisfactory—the sick attentively considered—the infirmary clean and free from any offensive smell and throughout the building the greatest order and attention. The management throughout reflects the highest credit on all concerned. I examined one or two children and heard them questioned by the schoolmistress. Their answers were satisfactory, they appear to be carefully instructed.

(Freemans Journal, 27 August 1849)

So the worst was over by the middle of 1849, but we must not underestimate the misery of the preceding years, which was to continue for several years yet. We now go back to those worst years to look in detail at the dreadful journeys our ancestors made to England, America, and Australia, leaving their precious families in order to seek a better life for themselves and their children in other lands.

8. Leaving for England—Patrick Lally

We now need to go back a few years, because we know that Patrick Lally had left Ireland and was in London by the autumn of 1847. Even if we believe he was not at the bottom of Irish society and didn't suffer as badly as many did, he and his family would still have been caught up in all the terrors just described and been in the rush to get out. Starvation, eviction, disease, and severe weather—by January 1847 all hope in Ireland was lost. Previous fears of the unknown abroad were cast aside because nothing could be worse than staying in the face of certain death. There began a great mobilisation of stick men, women, and children. From the west of Galway there was a stampede to the east and to large towns, and the land became almost entirely depopulated. The fear of leaving now turned to a fear of being left behind.

Many moved to Galway where even the prison, the only one in the county and built to house 5,000 inmates, now held 13,000 paupers. If Patrick was in Loughrea in February 1847 he would have seen the streets crowded with starving paupers trudging through in bare feet and a few rags in heavy snow. The mass moved on east, with the intention to get out across the Irish Sea to England, or better still, to America via Liverpool or Cork. America was beyond English control and there was freedom from the social and political gridlock that had killed Ireland. The canal boats were full, but most travellers could not have afforded them at any price so most looked forward to a journey of at least a week, on foot.

Emigrants receiving the priest's blessing
as they leave home.

An emigration agent's office

Many Irish men, particularly from the east, were familiar with the crossing to England. They went over as labourers to work on the new railways and ports which were largely constructed by cheap Irish labour. They also went over seasonally for the harvest. However, the new vast wave of people now gathering in Dublin, Cork and other smaller ports were unfamiliar with a city or travel or docks. They wouldn't know who to trust or how to get the best price for the sea crossing, but they crowded the docks desperate to get away.

In Dublin and Cork soup kitchens operated on an industrial scale with paupers queuing for hours to be let in ten at a time to drink, leave, and let the next ten in. Campaigners complained that such treatment was inhumane, worse than you would treat an animal, but how else could so many tens of thousands be served? In Cork over 30,000 pints of soup were served daily, and it was reported that this did not feed one tenth of those in need of it.

The soup kitchen in Dublin.

The Irish poor set sail for every port, small and large, in England, Scotland, and Wales. How did they get there, and how did they afford the fare? Many pawned everything they owned. A *Times* newspaper correspondent visited a pawnbrokers in Galway. Milk pails, stools, spades, and forks were there by the dozen as people pawned their whole Irish life for the fare out. He was amazed to find high-value coins and notes pawned for lesser amounts. Such things as sovereigns were not understood by people who used only barter. These would have been hidden in the thatch because the owner had an idea they were of value and might be useful one day. His biggest surprise was a Bank of Ireland £20 note that had been pawned for ten shillings (50p) because the owner couldn't spend the note but needed the small change for food and fare on his journey, from which he would probably never return.

The most common means of acquiring the fare was for a pauper family to be given it by their Poor Law Union. To get rid of a whole family for ten shillings (50p) was better than looking after them for five shillings (25p) a week. Priests handed out money as acts of charity as did some more benevolent landlords to get rid of tenants who would never be able to pay their rent. A crossing in a small coaster had normally been bought for two shillings and sixpence (12½p) but prices were now at rock bottom. Ironically the relief operation was at last getting under way and a great many food ships were plying the Irish Sea. They had been going back empty, but could now take on a human return cargo at prices down to a few pence. Some ship's captains were taking paupers over free because they were cheaper than loading lime or shingle as ballast. Human ballast walked on and off for nothing, but, as it was said at the time, they were packed in worse than pigs because pigs had a market value.

Liverpool docks from where many Irish sailed to America.

Liverpool, which already contained some of the worst slums in Britain, was by far the greatest recipient of this human cargo. The city population had grown rapidly to about 230,000, many of them Irish and working on the new Birkenhead and Albert Docks. In the last week in January 1847, 198,000 people received poor relief in Liverpool, and in the five months between January and May 300,000 Irish landed at the port.

They came off the ships exhausted, often sick and disorientated and easy prey for the touts, who were usually their own countrymen and who knew that the emigrants had on them all their worldly possessions and money for the onward journey from which, by trickery or violence, they could easily be parted.

Not all the travellers stayed as many went on as soon as they could on ships to North America and others dispersed throughout England. The City Council put a petition to parliament for aid to prevent the city from going bankrupt, but it was refused. The head constable of Liverpool sent two detective constables to Ireland to assess the situation, and their report caused outrage. They travelled in a loop from Dublin, through counties Roscommon, Sligo, Mayo, and Galway and reported that they encountered many thousands of destitute men, women, and children on the highway, all heading for the Irish east-coast ports and England.

The constables reported the reason for this flight to be because Irish paupers could only get assistance inside a workhouse in Ireland, many of which had not enough money to feed their inmates and some of which were closed. It was known that there was much better food to be had in English workhouses, and aid could be received outside the workhouse in England. The constables reported how these paupers were getting their fares. The ratepayers of Liverpool were shocked to learn that English money, given to feed the Irish poor, was being given to the poor so that they could sail to England where English money would pay again to look after them.

The constables' descriptions of hundreds of evictions pending in every court demonstrated that the wave of refugees was not going to decline. In Ballinrobe, 50 miles northwest of Loughrea, 6,000 applications for rent had been made at just one Quarter Sessions in the one town, and nearly every one would result in an eviction. Liverpool, which had proudly been in the forefront of building and sanitary improvements, was facing ruin beneath a tidal wave of destitute Irish living packed together in cellars, attics, sheds, and under bridges without any belongings or sanitation.

Every other port from Glasgow south through Wales and all the small harbours round the coast to Falmouth and beyond experienced this wave of destitute humanity. In South Wales the numbers could not be counted because hostility to the Irish in the major ports led ships' captains to drop them off at tiny harbours along the coast or make them wade to beaches.

They then still made their way to the large cities and their cheap lodging houses and workhouses. Of course, they brought with them the fevers so prevalent at home. Attempts in many ports to turn away ships that carried fever sufferers only caused chaos as they lay at anchor outside, blocking the way of other ships.

This wave of new Irish immigrants spread inland and began to gather in large numbers in towns from Edinburgh, to York, Oxford, Bath, and beyond where there was nowhere to accommodate them. This unparalleled influx struck fear into the English public, not only because of the fevers but because they would take jobs at any price from local people. The state of Ireland was forcibly brought home to the English by dirty, emaciated strangers, some little better than naked, knocking on doors all over England begging for food, clothes, or money. And they were skilled beggars, not to be turned away easily. Worse still, they were found dead on beaches and in the streets. There was an outcry in the press and in Parliament as to how Britain, head of the mighty Empire, could allow such a thing in her own islands.

Of course, London was not immune from the Irish influx, and we know that by the autumn of 1847 our Patrick Lally was in London because his first son, James William, was born in London, to an English girl on 9 August 1848. How Patrick travelled from Loughrea to London is not now known, but he would certainly have been part of, or have witnessed, the new Irish arrivals in London in that year.

St Marylebone Poor Law Union reported that applications at their temporary night shelter, outside the workhouse, increased from 148 to 945 in the couple of months up to February 1847. By May 1,000 Irish paupers were said to be entering London each week, and the night shelter set up by Marylebone Workhouse had to be closed because so many Irish had the fever.

The Irish were declared a public nuisance as they lay down in the road outside the workhouse gates awaiting admission. They were unwelcome almost everywhere as they stole jobs by accepting the lowest wages, they brought disease, they harassed the locals with their begging, and they brought down whole neighbourhoods by living in overcrowded, insanitary conditions; the last being hardly surprising considering their typical way of life at home.

If Patrick was among this great crowd of poverty-stricken refugees he was soon to land on his feet. He met Elizabeth White from Isleworth, west of London, with whom he started a family, their first son being born in August 1848. He would marry Elizabeth in July 1851 and have nine children. By 1851 he was the gardener to Lord Ernest Bruce and, on the night of the 1851 census was the sole occupant of his Lordship's house in 'the village of Harlesden' and 'looking after the house'. He was in a trusted and responsible position, and, surely, Lord Bruce would not have given the sole care of his house to someone who fitted the image of the typical Irish immigrant so often portrayed at that time.

Patrick was pursuing his high hopes and plans for the future. Through the next twenty years he was a gardener, not a navvy or common labourer, and he went on to have his own mushroom farm in Kensington from which he supplied many of the large houses and businesses in west London. He dreamt of, or was involved in, speculation in the Swan River in Western Australia, but this came to nought.

After such a promising beginning, Patrick's fortunes in England went downhill. The hardships and eventual disappointments of life led him to a fondness for the bottle and a proneness to gambling in the hope of luck coming his way just this once. At some point around the early 1870s he and his whole family were put out on the street. He split up with Elizabeth, and the last fifteen years of his life were spent in either Kensington Workhouse or dependant on the hospitality of The Sisters of Nazareth Home for the Catholic Aged Poor. Patrick died in Kensington Workhouse in 1895, a year after Elizabeth.

The children of Patrick Lally and Elizabeth.

James William	1848
George Thomas	1851
John	1852
Joseph Ignatius	1854
Sarah Anne	1855
Mary Lucy	1856
Eliza Ann	1859
Agatha Mary	1860
Patrick Aloysius	1862

9. Leaving for North America—Patrick and Mary Lally

How many Irish emigrated in these few years of the Great Famine is not known. 'Over one million died and over one million emigrated' are the figures usually bandied about. But at least one respected authority, Cecil Woodham-Smith, estimates that one and a quarter million went to the USA and Canada and more than that went to the British mainland. Perhaps another quarter of a million went elsewhere—to Australia, South America, etc. There may be double counting, but the real total has to be near two million emigrants in four or five years. Patrick was just one of this vast crowd, and now we'll look at some other Lallys who emigrated from Loughrea. First we'll look at another Patrick Lally who left for the USA with his wife, Bridget, and son, also called Patrick. Then we'll look at the three Lally girls who left for Australia as orphans from Loughrea Workhouse. Their plight and stories complete the picture of what life was like for our family then and touches on their later lives.

This was a time when travel by sea was dangerous and not to be undertaken lightly. Shipwrecks were reported weekly in the press with lurid details and illustrations of the terrors of passengers and crew as their ship foundered or with fantastic imaginings of what may have happened to ships that disappeared without trace. The fear of those who boarded ships that they may never reach their destination was a real one. Icebergs, fire, and fever were the greatest threats besides simply foundering on rocks through storm or poor navigation. There were few regulations on shipping, and overcrowding was common. No ships carried enough lifeboats for all their passengers; some had just enough for those in cabins. If a ship went down on rocks, lifeboats were of little use. If it went down due to fire or storm miles from the shore it would be a remote chance that a lifeboat would ever be found.

Emigrants waiting on the quay at Cork.

An emigrant ship leaving Cork.

Emigrant ships were tiny by today's standards, and perhaps the best way to describe their size would be to imagine one placed on an imaginary modern tennis court. The court itself is 78 feet (23.8 metres) long. The standard distance between the base line and the high netting that surrounds the court is 21 feet (6.4 metres), making an overall length of 120 feet. These 120 feet were the length of a typical emigrant ship at the water line or on deck or in the steerage accommodation below decks; they were all much the same. The distance between the singles lines of a tennis court is 27 feet (8.2 metres) and this is the typical width of an emigrant ship. This tennis court is overlaid on the plan of the St Vincent shown on the following page. This plan was drawn for the *Illustrated London News* as she was preparing to load 240 emigrants plus crew for the journey to Australia. Imagine those people, perhaps 280 in total, standing on our imaginary tennis court. This number on a ship of this size was not unusual.

The relatively short passage across the Atlantic to North America had the worst survival record. A convict being sent to Australia had a much better chance of arriving alive and in good health. The reason for this was lack of regulation on the Atlantic routes leading to poor, cheap ship construction, bad state of repair, fewer crew, few doctors on board, and gross overcrowding. Taking on any passenger they could up to the day of sailing meant that ships took on fever too and that spread rapidly in the cramped conditions. Captains would take the shortest, northern route and risk icebergs and ice flows that could seize a ship, perhaps for weeks, or crush it to pieces. Regulations stated that the minimum provisions to be supplied were one pound per day (454 grams) per passenger. But one pound of what and for how many days? Passengers were advised to take their own food if they could, because a long delay meant hunger or thirst.

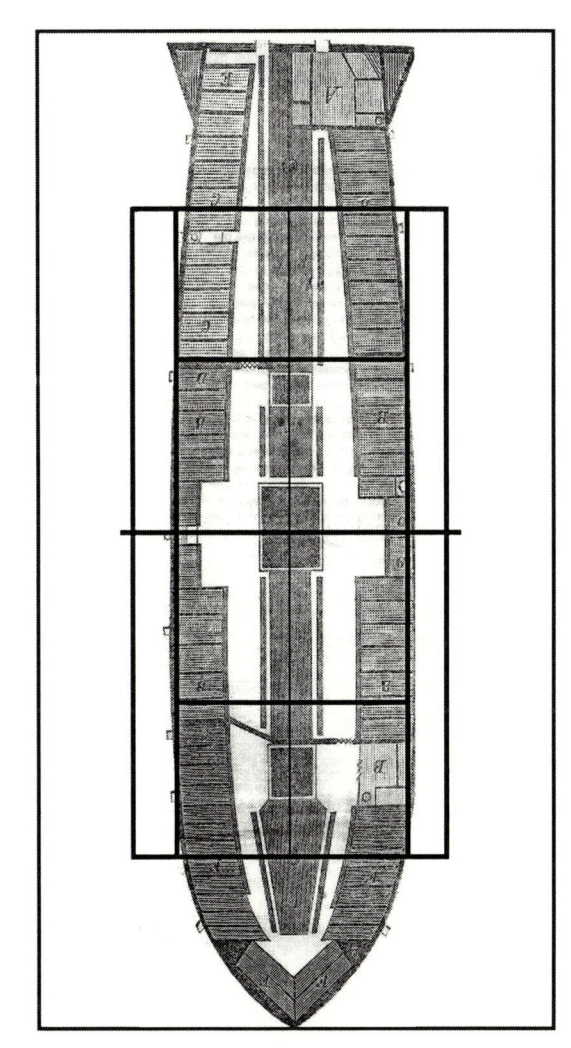

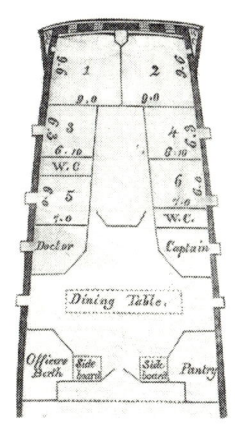

This shows the accommodation between decks on a typical emigrant vessel, the St Vincent, overlaid on a tennis court to demonstrate its size.

The ship is as long as the distance between the high nets at each end of the court and its width fits between the singles lines. It shows each emigrant's quarters and the tables down the middle.

On the right is a plan of the cabin accommodation. The largest cabins were nine feet six inches x nine feet (two metres) square. They were hardly spacious but offered a little privacy.

Conditions in steerage class on board were cramped, even with the correct complement of passengers. Their quarters were below deck at or just above the water line. Berths, or beds, were arranged down both sides, head outside, feet to the middle—bunks in two tiers. A standard berth measured 6 feet x 6 feet (183 x 183 centimetres), but this was divided in two so that each bed was 6 feet x 3 feet, and each bed took two people. So each berth held four people, each having a quarter. This was their 'quarters'. There was a flimsy partition between berths and space beneath the bottom bed for passengers' belongings. The overall height was about 6 feet 6 inches to 7 feet 6 inches (2 to 2.5 metres), so headroom in bed was perhaps a little over 2 feet (70 centimetres).

Washing, when done, was with bowls of water passed round or with a sea water shower on deck for men. Toilet facilities were perhaps two water closets, but most steerage passengers, particularly assisted emigrants whose passage was paid for by the government, had to be taught how to use them. Down the full length of the centre of the steerage level, ran a wide table with raised edges and fixed benches. Underneath was storage for pots, pans, plates, etc. Passageways on each side between bed and bench were about two feet (sixty-five centimetres) wide. When full there was very little space, and privacy did not exist. When the hatches above were battened down in bad weather, which could last for days, the situation inside must have been appalling and, when overcrowded, ten times worse.

These ships sailed badly and slowly. Their blunt prows didn't cut through the water but took every knock that the waves gave them with a shudder. They rode the waves like a cork, rising, falling, and rocking with every wave. They leaked continuously and needed constant pumping. The constant noise of creaking timbers and the sea was deafening. To an Irish family from Loughrea who had perhaps never seen a ship before, all this was terrifying. Add to this the overcrowding, seasickness, fever, hunger, and thirst, and these ships became hell-holes.

* * *

A scene between decks.

Sitting in their quarters in steerage.

Our next example of flight from Loughrea is another Patrick Lally who left before the Great Famine and the rush it created, so he would not have experienced the worst of this journey. His father was called Patrick and his son too. Despite Irishmen commonly having the nickname of Pat or Paddy, the name Patrick was not a dominant boys' name in Ireland. This Patrick was born in Loughrea on 15 March 1817. His father, Patrick, was born in 1790, and his mother, Bridget (née Farrell), was born in 1795, and we know that he had at least two brothers, Matthew, who was born on 20 January 1816, and John. Patrick senior and Bridget married in St Brendan's Cathedral in Loughrea on 2 April 1815. Patrick junior, the one who left for America, married Mary Elizabeth Byrne in 1840.

Patrick was a school teacher in Loughrea but probably had no teaching qualifications, which, judging by what we have already seen of the schools at that time, was perhaps not unusual. His reason for leaving Loughrea was that he was wanted by the police. It is believed he was a revolutionary, and he emigrated in a hurry in May 1843, before the Great Famine. There were many reasons why a man could be wanted by the police, but the fact that he had to leave suggests it was something more serious than damaging crops or burning property, the sort of thing that happened in response to the frustration and impotence associated with unjust evictions or rising food prices. Patrick, being a schoolteacher, could have been quite easily traced, as he would have had a known home and place of work and, unlike a labourer or farmer, couldn't easily find work secretly elsewhere. A spell in prison would ruin his career.

So many Irish emigrants sailed across the Atlantic, undoubtedly including some of our Lallys, that it is worth covering the story of emigrants to North America in our story. Many whose aim was to reach the USA sailed via Canada.

Emigrants at dinner.

A ship's kitchen.

The British government was encouraging emigration to Canada by keeping sailing costs low by not legislating to raise standards on board. This was partly to build up the population of Canada in order to develop the land there but also due to a fear of mass Irish immigration into England that would depress wages and living standards and be a burden on the rates. By 1845 about 2,000 ships were plying that route from Britain, mainly bringing timber from Canada and taking passengers back. Even in 1843, before the rush, about 68,000 emigrated from Ireland of whom 21,000 went to Canada or via Canada. It cost only about £2 for the journey to Quebec compared with more than three times that price on an American ship going to New York, but American ships were much better and safer. In 1843, for example, when Patrick and Mary Lally sailed, seventeen British ships bound for Canada sank in the St Lawrence River alone with the loss of 731 lives.

But the Irish wanted to go to the USA, which was a thriving new economy full of real opportunities, compared with old, backward Canada. The USA was also free of British rule which would have been important to the fugitive Patrick and Mary. Once on board an American ship they would have been free, whereas Patrick might still have been in danger of arrest in British Canada even in the few days it would have taken him to get across the border into the USA.

They may have found their £4 fare for Canada from savings, but family and sympathisers could have got together the £12 to £15 needed to get direct to the USA in an emergency. The USA authorities had strict rules on who they let in to avoid British immigrants being a burden on the state, but most emigrants at this time were men or families who had a little capital and, as a teacher, Patrick would have had no problem.

Embarkation.

Roll call on the quarter deck.

Patrick and Mary settled in Dennison, Pennsylvania, about 100 miles inland from both New York and Philadelphia, but Patrick was unable to find work as a schoolteacher and ended up working in the coal mines. They had three daughters and two sons. Near him in the small settlement of Dennison was another Lally family, John and Bridget and their children. Is it a coincidence that a Patrick Lally and a John Lally lived so close to each other? The chances are that Patrick and John were brothers. Patrick died in 1874, aged fifty seven.

Patrick and Mary's 1843 Atlantic crossing may even have been pleasant if they sailed on an American ship, and even on a British ship they would have experienced nothing like the horrors of the scramble to leave Ireland a couple of years later. Within two years, such was the pressure to emigrate, that, for the first time ever, Atlantic shipping continued throughout the winter. Every possible ship was brought in to use whether suitable for the Atlantic voyage or not, and in 1846 they sailed from every tiny unregulated harbour on the west coast of Ireland, such as Sligo, Westport, Tralee, and Ballina.

Typical of these appropriately called 'coffin ships' was the *Elizabeth and Sarah* which sailed from Killala where the harbour offered safe anchorage only to ships drawing up to nine feet of water. This ship was tiny, only 330 tons, so not a lot longer than the distance between the base lines of a tennis court. She was seventy-four years old, yet she sailed with 276 passengers, only two-thirds of the legal minimum amount of drinking water, in rotten casks, and hardly any food. Few of the passengers had any food to take with them. The voyage took seventy-two days, not an untypical duration, during which time they ran ashore on a reef but managed to refloat. There were no sanitary arrangements and the state of the vessel was described on arrival as, 'horrible and disgusting beyond the power of language to describe'. The captain died during the voyage, and the ship with its starving crew and passengers

Departure.

had to be towed into the St Lawrence River by a steam tug. It's surprising that only forty-two died on this voyage. This sailing had been put together by Irish speculators who sold tickets to desperate customers at inflated prices.

Another scandal was the cheap passages bought by landlords. One of the worst cases concerned about 2,000 tenants shipped from the Strokestown estates of Viscount Palmerston, the British Foreign Secretary. Strokestown is about fifty miles north of Loughrea. Lord Palmerston's tenants made up a large proportion of the passengers on nine ships that sailed from the tiny harbour at Sligo. To take one ship as an example, the *Lord Ashburton* carried 477 passengers of whom 107 died on the voyage. The crew was incapable of finishing the voyage and five passengers managed to bring the ship into the St Lawrence River. One hundred and seventy-four passengers were from Lord Palmerston's estates of whom eighty-seven of the survivors had to be clothed from Canadian public money before they could, with decency, leave the ship. Care of nearly all the Strokestown passengers in the nine ships fell on the Canadian public purse as none had the £1 promised by Lord Palmerston to set themselves up in their new life. The Canadian government made a public complaint to Lord Palmerston to which he merely forwarded a letter from his Irish land agent, which was considered by the governor general of Canada to be insolent. In summary, his agent's answer included points such as: why would Lord Palmerston spend money sending anybody of any use to a foreign land, so what did the Canadians expect? As for sending them naked to a Canadian winter, clothes had been supplied of the quality they normally wore. It was the likes of Lord Palmerston who, like Lord Lucan, brought the lasting hatred of many Irish on the whole British people.

In 1847 typhoid fever was wracking the poor in Ireland and this spread rapidly to the emigrant ships. The quarantine hospital on Grosse Isle at the mouth of the St Lawrence River had 300 beds. By the end of May 1847, 1,100 patients were accommodated at Grosse Isle, many in tents and lying in the church. Forty ships were at anchor waiting to offload their cases of fever and dysentery. By July the queue of ships waiting without food or water was miles long, and it was estimated that 20,000 to 25,000 passengers should be in quarantine. There were 2,500 in the hospital, and conditions were filthy, unsanitary, verminous, and out of control. Twelve of the fourteen medical staff were ill; many doctors died; and nurses were unobtainable.

Hundreds died of fever in the camps set up for the healthy. Quarantine was virtually abandoned as fever was carried to towns and cities in Canada and the USA. The Anglican bishop of Toronto and the mayor of Montreal were among hundreds of indigenous Canadians who died caring for the sick. The conditions on board and the length of time these inadequate ships took on the Atlantic crossing, frequently three months, meant the death rate was enormous. For example, 427 passengers were squeezed on to the 495 ton *Agnes* and

190 died on the voyage or in quarantine. Over 100,000 Irish emigrants sailed for Canada in 1847, the exact number being impossible to know, but records tell us that about 17,000 died on the voyage and 20,000 soon after arrival.

The USA authorities saw all this coming and did everything they could to prevent the Irish from landing at American ports. They passed Passenger Acts that increased fares and demanded bonds from ships' captains that no passenger would be a liability to the state. They physically repelled ships that had fever on board, even with starving passengers who faced the prospect of several days sailing north to a British Canadian port. Although successful collections for the starving Irish in Ireland were made by American Irish and Christian groups, the general public agreed with these harsh measures.

There was strong anti-British and anti-Catholic sentiment and a great fear that British low wages would be imported by men who would work for virtually nothing and steal jobs from resident Americans. Riots broke out to protect jobs and against popery even before the rush of 1845, the most serious being in Philadelphia in 1844. There were outcries at the quality of the Irish who made it to America and claims that Britain was casting out the lowest of its society to be looked after at American expense. Many immigrants were women and children, the old, idiots, cripples, and even blind and many of the so-called able-bodied were not fit for manual labour. Nevertheless, many thousands of Irish did make it in, some to be picked up by 'runners', their own countrymen, who promised them accommodation and work but in fact robbed them of everything they had. Many Irish, having taken too many of life's hard knocks, could be seen emaciated, half naked and begging on the streets of American cities for several years later.

Such events would have formed the background to the lives of all the Irish. In the five years from 1846 to 1850, 180 Lallys were recorded as arriving in the USA, and many more would have sailed on the cheap to Canada. Those who survived would have written home so stories of these events must have affected the lives of their families back in Ireland. The natural fear of families saying farewell to loved ones was that they would never see or hear from them again. Many never did receive a letter, perhaps because their relatives ended their journey at Grosse Isle. The anti-Catholic riots in Philadelphia must have been too close for comfort for Patrick and Mary and perhaps were one of the reasons he failed to get a teaching job. It's all part of the Irish cauldron from which we Lallys have emerged.

10. Leaving for Australia—Mary Anne, Margaret and Mary Lally

Fewer emigrants went to Australia in this scramble to get away because of the cost and because the distance meant few could even dream of ever coming back. However, the long journey was a lot less risky than the simple trip across the Atlantic, largely because these sailings were controlled by the government and there was not the overcrowding or the use of inadequate ships. Three young Lally girls from the Loughrea area made this trip, and it is interesting to look at their experiences because of the chance that they were our cousins.

Mary Anne, age sixteen, and Margaret Lally, age fourteen, were sisters. Their parents, Martin and Eliza Lally, were dead by 1848, and the girls had been in the Loughrea Workhouse. They had at least one brother, John, but at only about nine years old he was too young to go with them and boys were not included in the scheme under which they went. On the same ship went fifteen-year-old Mary Lally from Ballymacward just north of Kiltullagh but in the Ballinasloe Poor Law Union. Her parents, Patrick and Miriam Lally, were both dead. Other than their parents' names, nothing is known of these girls or their families before they entered the workhouse. They were orphans, and it is not known how closely Mary was related to the other two.

These girls lived through hell in 1848, but their lives thereafter were to be transformed beyond their wildest imaginings. The chances are that they witnessed their parents dying of starvation or disease brought about by the famine and perhaps some brothers and sisters too. It is not known when the two girls entered Loughrea Workhouse, built for 800 inmates,

Loughrea Workhouse, south of the town and next to the lake.

but by the time they left for Australia on 28 October 1848 it held over 2,000 paupers. Perhaps they were there before February 1848 when the Board of Guardians was replaced for incompetence, failure to collect the Poor Rates, and because of the appalling conditions, described earlier. Signs of these dreadful conditions can be seen in the records for the year earlier when, in three weeks in March 1847, the matron resigned because she couldn't cope, the medical officer resigned due to his own ill health and a new schoolmaster left after his first day. Such conditions could not be improved overnight, particularly when numbers were rising so rapidly, so life for Mary Anne and Margaret Lally must have been dreadful. Just three weeks before they left the decision had been made to take over the redundant brewery and several empty houses in Bride Street, so in their last weeks they would have seen the upheaval of moving nearly 1,000 men out to the new buildings.

The girls travelled under the government-sponsored Earl Grey Scheme, which was set up both to solve Irish overpopulation and because at this time there was great demand from Australia for new emigrants, particularly single girls because of the disproportionate number of men in the colony. Of the convicts sent there, 85 per cent were men. Also, men were much more likely to emigrate than women. Assisted emigration schemes were not new and should not be seen as solely an Irish programme. Schemes had begun in 1829, not only to relieve poverty and overcrowding in Britain but also to establish and expand the British population and influence in the colonies.

This, of course, fitted in well with the problems in Ireland, particularly after the worst year of the famine, 1847, when Poor Law Boards were concerned about the on-going costs of looking after thousands of orphaned children. The Earl Grey Scheme was for Irish girls only and offered a double benefit of reducing the excess population in Ireland and providing women as domestic servants and to facilitate the building of families and a stable society in the vast free lands of Australia.

It was a short lived scheme, its closure being announced in the House of Commons in March 1850:

> *In consequence of the events of the last two years the Commission has come to the conclusion that it is not desirable as a general rule to undertake the emigration of orphan girls from workhouses having due regard to the welfare and safety of the girls themselves.*

That's interesting, and we shall look at the danger to our girls' welfare and safety later. In May 1850 it was announced in the House of Lords that all such schemes would end for boys as well as girls and that between 1847 and 1850 a total of 44,093 children had been sent out from British workhouses, 20,553 boys and 23,440 girls, including 4,128 girls from Ireland (*Times, 29* May 1850).

As harsh as it may seem now to ship these poor, little girls to the ends of the earth there was a responsible paternalism at the heart of the scheme, and this was echoed by the Loughrea Board of Guardians, if not by all such boards. The girls had entered the workhouse because they had nobody to support them and nowhere else to go, but they were then under the control of the Board of Guardians who could direct them to do certain activities and to go where the guardians saw fit. In Loughrea Workhouse there was a positive attitude to encouraging emigration and the care of the girls was considered paramount as was shown by the following statement, recorded in the Loughrea Guardians' Minute Books on 21 October 1848. All requests to the Loughrea Guardians for assisted emigration were accepted but all requests to the Ballinasloe Guardians at the end of 1848 were refused, perhaps because they didn't want to spend the money.

> *Resolved: That we deem it a matter of incalculable advantage to the Union to promote by any means the emigration of some considerable numbers of paupers who are now crowding the Workhouse, not only as a means of providing for the most deserving of those persons but also for the ultimate relief of the Union. And as Mr Henry, Emigration Agent, has recently lately selected from among the female orphans of this house a list of 48 deserving objects for emigration to South Australia and the Poor Law commissioners having sanctioned their being forwarded, we hereby consent to provide them with the necessary outfit as decided upon by the Emigration Commissioners.*

This paragraph may have been recorded to ingratiate the relatively new guardians with the Poor Law Commissioners because preparations had been going ahead for several weeks. The Emigration Commissioners laid down strict criteria by which girls may qualify to go and also gave a list of clothing and equipment the local workhouse was to supply for them.

They had to be fourteen years old or more, have no parents alive, be of exemplary character and behaviour, able to read, write and do arithmetic, be carefully trained in useful industry, particularly of a domestic nature, familiar with the principles of the Christian religion, healthy, and have had smallpox or been inoculated. On the day the girls left there was a total of 466 girls in the workhouse. Despite so-called universal education since 1831, only about a third of girls could read and write. Add the other criteria of age, health etc. and it is likely that all eligible girls were selected so one has to wonder whether they were given the choice.

But it was presented to the girls as an honour to be chosen for such an opportunity and they probably needed little persuading. By this time word had come back from previous emigrants that told of the Australian life. While it may be harsh, they could cope with that because Australia also offered great wages, accommodation, and food in plentiful supply. There would be people at their destination to welcome them, look after them, and get them placed in suitable jobs. At this time, no doubt, the possible emotional problems and loneliness were not explained. Immediate benefits would have been obvious, starting with their 'wardrobe', the richness of which must have amazed them.

The fact that the preparations for the girls' departure is recorded in detail not found elsewhere in the Minute Books suggests, to me, an interest in the operation and a willingness to do what was right for them. On 30 September the Loughrea Guardians approved orders for the girls' wardrobe, detailing the ladies or tailors who were to make certain quantities of each item and the prices and qualities. Bearing in mind the regular orders for cloth, thread, needles, etc. for the workhouse these items could perhaps have been made more cheaply by the inmates. But this was not the case. The following was ordered.

86 gowns	at between 5½d (2p) and 2/4 (12p) per yard, made up.
48 cloaks	at between 8/6 and 16/6
38 neckerchiefs	at between 5½d and 1/11
106 shawls	at between 3/6 and 5/11
49 stays	at between 2/11 and 3/4
144 pairs of stockings	at 6d and 6½d
48 bonnets	not priced
150 yards of ribbon	at 6d and 6½d
80 towels	not priced
48 brushes	at 1/-
48 backcombs	at 1½d
48 tooth combs	at 4½d

What treasure chests for pauper girls. What wasn't ordered in multiples of forty eight was probably made up from workhouse stock. The emigration commissioners also stated that such items as shoes, mitts, soap, a Bible, and Prayer Book must be given to the girls along with 'Needles, thread, tape, etc and other little articles (such as cotton and calico) the matron may know young females to require' and we can be sure these items were added. It was stipulated that all this was to go in a wooden box, measuring twenty-four inches x fourteen inches x fourteen inches (sixty x thirty-six x thirty-six centimetres) with their name on the lid and list of contents inside the lid. The contract for the forty-eight boxes went to Mr Joseph O'Brian at a cost of 6/6 each. That was not a cheap box!

But from here the Loughrea Board of Guardians seem to have gone further than the minimum requirements. On 7 and 14 October orders were agreed for those 'other little articles (such as cotton and calico)'. This list was a wagon load in itself.

413½ yards grey Calico
216 yards black Calico
4½ yards of linen
1 piece of long cloth
40 pieces of white tape
6 pieces of black tape
2 dozen tape

½ lb white thread
300 needles
12 dozen Cording
56 dozen hooks and eyes
96 cotton balls

The girls would not have bothered themselves with the cost. Their journey from Plymouth to Australia which cost about 14 guineas (£14.70) was paid from colonial funds and their workhouse was to provide this clothing and equipment and pay for their passage under supervision to Plymouth. The crossing to Plymouth cost about 10/6 (55p) and official estimates stated that the total cost to the workhouse should not exceed £5. This was a very considerable amount of money compared with the 10d (4p) a day considered a fair wage for a labourer and the 4d a day they were prepared to work for. Put against the 1/3½ (8p) a week it cost to keep each girl it was not looked at as a commercial proposition but was done largely for benevolent reasons and as an attempt at a long-term cure for the problems of Ireland. Something had to be done, and was.

At the last minute the Emigration Commissioner reduced the number of paupers to be despatched from forty eight to forty, which must have been devastating to the eight taken out of the party. These eight left exactly a month later and further departures brought the total from Loughrea under the Earl Grey Scheme to seventy three.

So, on Thursday, 26 October 1848, the party of girls climbed aboard wagons at the Loughrea Workhouse gate and were waved off by friends and relations who they would never see again. Mary Anne and Margaret and nine-year-old brother, John, who was to stay behind, must have shed many a tear as they left with promises to send for him when they'd made their fortune. Slowly they made their way beyond the only countryside familiar to them since birth. In charge of the party was Mr Miller, the workhouse master.

Emigrants' farewell.

The girls cannot have been able to imagine what was in store for them. The amazing sights they would see, the fantastic modes of transport, the frightening speeds, and the sheer distance they would travel may have been described to them, but they wouldn't have grasped the enormity of it all. Were they excited or frightened, happy or in tears? Certainly all those emotions and more.

Although they were in the care of the workhouse master, our sisters, Mary Anne and Margaret, were now moving into the control of the Emigration Commissioners who were moving numerous groups from across Ireland to one destination. The wagons took them to Ballinasloe where they almost certainly met the party from Ballinasloe Workhouse, including Mary Lally. Here they were booked on a passage boat on the Grand Canal.

These boats were fifty-two feet (sixteen metres) long by nine feet ten inches (three metres) wide and divided into state

146

saloons, seating forty five, and common cabins, seating thirty five. There was a galley in the centre where meals were prepared and a fireplace in each cabin. There was nowhere to sleep so the state passengers slept on the pillows supplied, resting their heads on the boat side or on the table that ran down the centre. The common passengers on their wooden benches slept where they could or climbed onto the deck on the roof where they slept in the open air. The main route for emigrants was to Dublin and most, in the unhurried days before the mid-1840s, would have travelled on the Grand Canal. Even then the boats were frequently overcrowded, and during the rush to get out during the Great Famine these boats were packed on the journey east.

The girls would have more than taken up the whole of a common cabin, and with the crowds of other emigrants heading east, the Grand Canal Company wouldn't have bothered about limiting the number in the Common Cabin to thirty five. They probably met there other groups from Galway workhouses so the parties combined could have booked a boat to themselves. Surely all that luggage would have gone ahead separately. Maybe they went, with their luggage, in a freight boat, although their fare of 5/6, compared with a standard passenger fare of 6/-, would suggest they didn't travel that cheaply. Whatever happened, Mr Miller would have been hard pressed to safeguard and shepherd his girls and get them all safely on board the boat they had booked. At the end of October they would have all wanted to be inside, never mind how packed it was, rather than on the roof.

The standard night boat service left at 3 p.m. with an expected arrival at Sallins at 10.45 the following morning—a journey of seventy-five miles taking over fifteen hours through the night. Here was the girls' first new and strange experience. Even getting into a boat would have presented its fears and the banging against lock sides would have upset them at first. They joined the main canal at the River Shannon, and

An Irish canal.

here their boat would have been hauled across the wide river by winches and pulleys. The end of the journey, into Sallins, was across the Leinster Aqueduct, which, although not very high as aqueducts go, may have seemed to them like flying. They may well have wondered if this is what it would be like crossing the Pacific Ocean.

The reason their canal journey stopped at Sallins, nineteen miles from Dublin, was that the railway west from Dublin had reached there two years earlier. The Grand Canal journey from here to Dublin took another four and a half hours because of all the locks but the train took forty-five minutes. There was, of course, the need to transfer girls and cargo from boat to train, but the system was set up for this and Mr Miller would have made sure it went well.

Any girl brave enough to go and look at the steam locomotive would have been in for another unbelievable and frightening new experience. For country girls who had not seen anything bigger or faster than a Bian the locomotive and its carriages would have been a fearsome, almost living and breathing, monster. Do not underestimate the awe and fear it would have produced in a fourteen-year-old girl in 1848. Railways were the very latest technology, creating investment fever and set to change the world rapidly. Eighteen forty eight was only twenty-three years after the inauguration of the world's first passenger railway from Stockton to Darlington. It was only ten years after the completion of the main line from London to Birmingham and two years since a line reached Holyhead to connect with the fast steam boats to Dublin.

Waiting at an Irish station.

This time was the height of 'railway mania' when, in 1846, 272 Acts were passed by Parliament allowing railway building. But with over 1,700 miles of railway built in Great Britain at this time, only about 100 miles existed in Ireland, and all on the east coast. In Ireland, in 1846 The Great Southern and Western Railway had ordered twenty of the latest six wheel 'Express' locomotives from the company of Bury, Curtis and Kennedy of Liverpool, and it was one of these that was in Sallins station. The driving wheels were 5 feet 8 inches (1.73 metres) in diameter, taller than most Irish men, the top of the boiler was 7 feet 8 inches (2.34 metres) and the funnel was

149

way up at 11 feet 6 inches (3.50 metres), towering over the girls. The whole creature, including the coal and water tender, was about 35 feet (10.7 metres) long and 6 feet 6 inches (2 metres) wide. These were the very latest locomotives and the pride of the company. The standard of workmanship was superb, and they were kept in outstanding condition with gleaming brass and copper—even the enormous domed copper fire box was polished till it shone—immaculate paint and varnish, and moving parts oiled, greased, and cleaned daily. This fearsome thirty-three ton hot and quietly pulsating machine waiting in Sallins station would have exuded power and wonder to anybody seeing it, let alone our girls from the quiet fields of the west.

A crowd waiting to board the train.

The girls climbed up two steep steps into heavy, wooden, third or fourth-class carriages, the floor of which was at about 4 feet (1.2 metres), above the wheels. They squeezed in five abreast on wooden bench seats, thirty girls to a carriage. There was only the barest protection from the elements. They soon gathered speed to over thirty miles per hour and the shaking and rocking, the noise and wind would have terrified some and thrilled others. From their high vantage point they could see for miles as the countryside rushed passed, and in forty-five minutes they were at Kingsbridge Station in the centre of Dublin.

Arriving at the station at about 2 p.m. on the Friday after a thirty-hour journey by cart, barge, and train the girls must have been exhausted and confused. They then had to travel a final two miles to North Wall Quay on the River Liffey from where the City of Dublin Steam Packet Company ran their regular services to Bristol, Plymouth, and France. The journey from the city centre with its grand buildings and bustling crowds could only have added to their bewilderment. Everything was so much bigger than in Loughrea. They probably transferred straight to their steamship, the *Duke of Cambridge*, which was waiting and due to sail the following day, on Saturday, 28 October.

Steamships waiting to set sail.

The *Duke of Cambridge* was a wooden paddle steamer, 158 feet (58 metres) long and 23 feet (8.4 metres) wide—long and thin,—built in 1837 at Glasgow. At eleven years old she was already dated. In the early 1830s, for example, steamships took seven to eight hours to sail the mail route from Dublin to Holyhead, but by the late 1840s this time had been halved. When new, the *Duke of Cambridge* would have been considered a fast boat, but in the three years prior to 1848, seventeen new fast, iron-paddle steamers had been brought into service on these routes. The *Duke of Cambridge* had been mainly used on the Dublin to Liverpool run where speed was not as important, and the national *Freeman's Journal*, in its society column, often reported the arrival or departure of important people on her. But in January 1840 she was

A steamship out at sea.

advertised as carrying, among other things, a cargo of champagne and wine from Le Havre. She was the ship advertised in the poster for pleasure cruises in July 1848 and may have been the ship used on the company's regular run to Plymouth. A main purpose of these ships was to carry livestock, which went below decks from where they couldn't be swept away in bad weather. Some ships had a few cabins, but steerage passengers were carried on deck, except those in the know who got downstairs quickly and snuggled down with the animals for warmth. So the *Duke of Cambridge* was a general purpose ship, ideal for a party of emigrant girls, now numbering a total of 164.

At this point Mr Miller handed over his responsibilities, and the orphan girls came under the care of the emigrant commissioners. Their last link with home said 'Goodbye', started his journey back to Loughrea, and the girls were finally on their own in strange surroundings and with strange company.

I like to think that this large party, with their guardians, had the ship to themselves. Surely, with the journey to Plymouth likely to take thirty hours they could go below deck without the company of animals and, judging by the girls' treatment elsewhere, this must have been the case. With all their luggage, there can't have been much room for any more passengers or cargo. It is unlikely they had ever seen a ship before, many would have been seasick, and these first days and nights at sea would have been very frightening and uncomfortable. But they travelled in considerably greater comfort than the hordes of their countrymen who were still crossing in large numbers.

Arriving in Plymouth on Monday, 30 October, the girls would have been travelling with very little break for four or five days. They were far from home, would surely have been weak, exhausted, and disorientated and, at the end of October, wet and cold. So just stop reading this interesting story for a moment and consider the reality for these girls. It must have been dreadful, and their journey had only just started. What had they let themselves in for?

Two barques at low tide.

At Plymouth they rested for a few days in the Government Emigration Depot, which had only the previous year been established in converted warehouses on the wharf. The girls had medical inspections and attended divine service before their departure. They were not alone as Plymouth was the rapidly growing major point of embarkation to Australia and New Zealand. About two ships were leaving each week, and in the port at that time were six ships other than theirs all preparing to sail for Australia with emigrants. Their ship, the *Inchinnan*, had only been built four years previously in Sunderland and had been sailing to and from the east: Bombay, Calcutta, Shanghai. This was to be her first trip to Australia. She was a 565 ton barque, a general purpose ship with three masts, and one of the smallest in port, a little smaller than the *St Vincent*, described earlier as just fitting in a tennis court. The girls' third means of water transport was a complete contrast to the previous two. As we have seen, these ships sailed badly, bobbing on the water like a cork, with constant movement, juddering, creaking, and noise despite not having engines. The *Inchinnan* was to be their home at sea for up to four months, depending on weather, currents, and skill of the crew.

In all, 164 girls sailed on the *Inchinnan* after four days in Plymouth. To care for them was a surgeon superintendent, Dr Ramsey, with his wife and small son and the matron, Eliza Hickey, with her husband and five daughters aged from ten to nineteen. There were two assistant matrons, one single and the other a widow with her young son, and four of the matron's daughters were also assistants. So there were eight adults to look after the 164 girls. In addition were six married emigrant couples in steerage, all farm labourers, and three other adults in cabins. All the passengers were Irish. Captain of the ship was Henry Pearce with thirty crew. In all, 233 souls sailed on the tide on Saturday, 4 November 1848, and 234 arrived in Sydney as Catherine Hannan was born on the voyage. What a difference to the coffin ships sailing across the Atlantic.

Towing out.

Theirs was the fourth Irish orphan ship to sail under the Earl Grey Scheme. Two had already arrived at their destinations, but nobody in Britain yet knew of the furore that resulted from the arrival of the first ship, the *Earl Grey*, in Sydney in October. The thousands of poor young women who had previously come to Australia had not created a good impression. There had already been several scandals involving emigrant girls in previous schemes. For example, earlier in 1848 on the *Subraon*, girls were plied with drink and taken to the crew's quarters. One girl had been hoisted up to the top of the main mast by a rope as a punishment, had a love affair with the chief mate, and died after an attempted abortion. No wonder there was concern for the girls' welfare.

There was a long history of shipping orphans to Australia, and all girls had been tarred with the same brush as the few bad ones who had been most noticeable. The general perception was that they were drunks, criminals, prostitutes and, if Irish, papists, and the *Earl Grey* delivered 200 of them in one go; 200 pubescent girls who had been cooped up in a small ship for 125 days and allowed to run riot. Australia needed immigrants, but what the Australian public hoped for, dreamed of, was young ladies. But single, young ladies did not travel alone around the world and what they got were tough, street-wise, foul-mouthed, traumatised girls from workhouses in the Belfast area. The surgeon and matron of the Subraon had lost control early on, and even they argued between themselves, and with the crew.

The behaviour of some of the girls had been so bad on board that they were immediately dispersed inland instead of staying fairly close to their port of arrival where they could be supervised and cared for as had been planned. Those that remained were not considered suitable for domestic service, perhaps because they had never known what a home was. When the news got back to Britain the row that followed and the public enquiry into how such girls were sent was to be the main reason for the ending of the scheme in 1850.

A vital fact that came out, too late, in the enquiry was the reception which greeted the second ship, the *Roman Emperor*, which arrived in Adelaide two weeks after the *Earl Grey* had reached Sydney. These girls from the same areas of the north of Ireland were greeted with open arms, rapidly placed into employment, and the lieutenant governor of South Australia said they could have placed 200 more. But the surgeon and matron on the *Roman Emperor* had maintained control and discipline. The matron had loaded materials, wools, and cotton to occupy the girls. The first thing the girls had to do was name tag all their clothing so there was no stealing and arguing. There was compulsory education in the three Rs and domestic matters throughout the voyage. There was absolutely no mixing of crew and girls. The *Roman Emperor's* voyage was only 89 days whereas the girls were on the *Earl Grey* for 125. The girls who arrived at Adelaide were more controlled, educated, and employable, and perhaps we can assume that the same could be said for girls from Loughrea, who took with them all those fabrics to keep them usefully employed and well controlled on their journey.

Mary Anne, Margaret, and Mary were oblivious to all this because they set sail less than a month after the *Earl Grey* had arrived, and the news would not have got back to England by then. They would most likely have had a day or two on board before sailing, and if the matron was wise, she would have set out the rules from the start by allocating berths to prevent arguments, for example. On the *Inchinnan* there was a cleaning rota and lights were to be out by 10 p.m. so we know some regulation was in place, and matron would have tried to establish a routine for eating, lessons, handiworks, etc.

On Saturday, 4 November, the wind was a fair breeze from the northwest, so it was ideal for their journey southwest and then south-southwest towards Spain. Without doubt all the girls would soon be struck down with seasickness, probably lasting about four days, and this would have been the worst time for them, especially if they hit bad weather in the Bay of Biscay, which was frequent in November, and the crew had to batten down the hatches. The violent movement of the ship, the cramped conditions, noise, dark, smell, water pouring in, and fear would have tested the girls' endurance, although there was no turning back now. When the vessel was tacking across the wind it wasn't unusual for the decks to be sloping at an angle of forty-five degrees, so even simple tasks like sewing or queuing at the pantry for daily rations were fraught with danger. It would have been a busy time for the surgeon and the matrons.

All ships to Australia had a surgeon-superintendant and Dr Ramsey was a fully qualified doctor. The matron would report to him and her duties involved the supervision of the girls, their education, occupation of their time and discipline. His responsibility was the health of the girls in all respects from curing illness to ensuring proper diet, cleanliness, and exercise. Most common complaints were diarrhoea, constipation, lice, common aches, pains and colds, and treating minor injuries. No doubt all the girls would have been well vetted for fever before sailing. The only major outbreak of disease Dr Ramsey reported was for four days in December. Nobody died, nobody was seriously ill and there was no fever.

Just as our girls were fortunate in their provision of a full wardrobe, so were they in their food on board. Under the Earl Grey Scheme they would have had a daily ration such as they had never seen before in quantity or variety: half a pound (227 grams) meat daily, a quarter of a pound (113 grams) flour, plus raisins, rice, tea, sugar, butter, and biscuit. Where were the potatoes? Some pigs and chickens would have been on board, probably on the deck and brought inside during rough weather for fear of them being swept away. In their spare moments the crew would have fished and this would have added variety, and excitement, especially if they managed to hook a shark. Their big challenge was to catch birds; an albatross made several good meals but such a prize wouldn't have been shared with the girls. The coal-fired cooking range was also on deck so would be out of action in bad weather but at such times it would be difficult to eat. The water taken on board would soon become foul so it was important to collect rainwater.

Something had to be done to overcome the tedium beyond belief which grew as the days passed. Even for our Irish girls who would have had little knowledge of timekeeping there was an isolation from reality. Matron would try to overcome this with a routine of getting up and going to bed, of lessons at set hours and organised amusements such as singing, acting in plays, and ladylike games. Without supervision the plays and songs would soon degenerate into coarseness and ribaldry. Somebody on board may have brought a musical instrument; a fiddle or flute perhaps. The journey would have been seen by the surgeon and matron as an opportunity for the girls' self improvement but to enthuse their charges would have been no easy task. None of their tasks was easy. The crew would have had their own amusements, no doubt unsuitable for the girls, and keeping the two sides apart must have been a constant battle. Once or twice a day there would have been prayers to the Almighty for deliverance from the perils of the sea; a suitable reminder of their predicament.

Time passed slowly on board as the Inchinnan made her way south down the coast of Africa where she was sighted by a homebound ship south of the equator. This would have caused great excitement as messages were passed by flags or, if close, by speaking trumpet. This encounter was reported when the other ship arrived in London and, as was customary, this appeared in the press as it would be the only news of the safety of any ship. The *Inchinnan* was on a government contract so would not have called into any port as she proceeded round the Cape of Good Hope with her young female cargo and out east across the vast Indian Ocean. These ships had only a rough idea of where they were at any time but, navigating by the stars, the *Inchinnan* reached the south coast of Australia and sailed through the dangerous 50 mile gap between King Island and Cape Otway where they would have seen Australia's first lighthouse, completed just a few months before. To achieve a time of less than 100 days to Sydney was real cause for celebration, the longest duration of these orphan ships being 147 days. The *Inchinnan's* was the second shortest voyage, arriving in just 101 days.

Safe and sound in port.

The previous description of life on board during these 101 days may mislead you into thinking this was an enjoyable voyage. It was not. With 164 young girls on board for nearly fifteen weeks this was no cruise. Susan Austen, the matron on the *Fitzjames* that left Plymouth eight years later left a diary of her experience revealing the constant fear and tension on board. She only had ninety five orphan girls but it is likely that she describes typical life on all these orphan ships. Here is her record, very much abridged, and for any twenty first century reader with experience of teenage girls it can only sound like a never-ending nightmare sleepover.

> *The seasickness. The precociousness and insolence of confident ringleaders asserting themselves. The creaking and groaning of timbers in the night and sudden irrational fears that spread mass panic. The false accusations, fighting and religious arguments. The confusion and screaming of abuse. The devil making work for idle hands. The boredom and refusal to attend lessons. The thieving, the pleadings of innocence against all the evidence, the cries of the aggrieved. The prayers of the Matron for God to give her strength. Calm days of a steady wind, the making of bonnets and new friendships. The tears of the timid and of the lonely for lost family and friends. Despair and fears of the unknown. The overpowering heat. The fear that drinking water will run out. The dreadful storms and the fear of death. The crying of the sick. Liaisons with the crew. The lack of sleep. The pulling of hair and pinching. The tantrums. The remembrance of those whose sweet nature endured through all provocation and temptation.*
>
> *'We are now at anchor and have had a safe passage and all have been well cared for, having been on board 15 weeks.'*
>
> *(NSW Archives)*

More insights into what life was like on board the *Inchinnan* came out in a court case when they arrived at Sydney, and this highlights contact between girls and crew which would have been officially frowned upon. Undoubtedly under the auspices of the Sydney Orphans Committee two of the *Inchinnan* girls brought a case against the chief officer, Alexander Taylor, for assault during the voyage. He was provoked into beating Mary Stephens—a fact—but did her injuries arise because of this or because she fell down the stairs on another occasion? He dragged Margaret Griffin across the deck because she wouldn't move—another fact. The evidence of the girls who appeared as witnesses was contradictory and unreliable. Despite weak evidence and good references from the captain and other passengers he had to be found guilty on both charges but the jury must have appreciated the duress he was under and requested he be treated mercifully by the court. Apparently he was short tempered and having to deal with insolent girls must have been too much for him. He was fined £5 on each charge for being a ruffian and for unmanly behaviour which must have been a large part of his pay for the trip.

However, during the trial the surgeon superintendant, Dr Ramsey, made comments that caused outrage and even caused questions to be raised in the House of Commons in London. His method of discipline was to dress errant girls in his trousers and parade them on the poop deck to the ridicule of the whole company. He wanted to hoist the worst girls up in the air by his belt to the yard arm but could not get the crew to do it. He saw nothing wrong with these punishments and mentioned them freely in court. It was this that reached the British press rather than details of the trial itself. Dr Ramsey defended himself in the press, quoting letters of commendation of his general attitude and compassion from the Matron and others, but to no avail. Such were the methods to try and maintain discipline, all of which would have been witnessed and talked about by Mary Anne, Margaret and Mary.

Life on board the *Inchinnan* was probably tedious and unpleasant but avoided most of the horrors of the Atlantic crossings. The *Inchinnan* and her 164 girls arrived at last on 13 February 1849 and the girls were welcomed by members of the government-sponsored Sydney Orphans Committee under the chairmanship of Frances Merewether, described as a caring and conscientious official. Other committee members brought a wealth of experience from the local Board of Guardians, Anglican,

Catholic and dissenting churches, the law, schools, and health care. Their aim was to ensure the welfare of the girls and their prompt employment and settlement. The girls were housed in the converted convict barracks near the port, government buildings and the principal Anglican and Catholic churches. Merewether was confident that the building offered 'every advantage that could be desired with reference to the health, the seclusion and the moral and religious instruction of the inmates and the convenience of persons coming to hire them.' The girls were, as must be expected, a true mix of characters and they had against them the general antagonism of the press and many of the public who gave them the character of the worst of their predecessors but in The Orphans Committee they had a safe haven.

The immigration records in Sydney record that fewer than half the girls arriving were able to read or write so assessment of this skill must have depended on the criteria used. In Australia Margaret and Mary were recorded as being able to read only and Mary Ann, the eldest at sixteen, was able to read and write.

The Orphans Committee set the terms under which the girls could be hired: their wages and a formal contract with commitment on both sides. The employer's responsibilities included instructing his apprentice in her tasks, feeding her properly, supplying specified lodgings, giving her time off, and taking care of her moral welfare. The girl had to be orderly and to act honestly and obediently to her master and his family, and keep his secrets. Obviously not everything turned out as orderly as was hoped: it doesn't in any situation. The girls had enormous adjustments to make to fit in to their new lives after all their recent traumas, and many new skills had to be learnt, often alone, away even from other friends they may have made on the journey. The girls were hired as apprentices with rates of pay, at £8 to £10 a year depending on age, well below that of skilled servants who could earn £17 to £28. This may have meant them being employed in families who had not had a servant before and had no idea of how to treat an employee. Any conflict could be reported back to the Orphan Committee by either side during the period of their apprenticeship which was two or three years, depending on the girl's age, and this facility may have encouraged complaints. Also, during this time the girl had to seek the permission of the committee to get married. The arrival and hiring of all immigrants was a matter of great interest in Sydney and regular reports appeared in the press of who had been hired, for what jobs and at what pay. *The Maitland Mercury* reported on 18 April, two months after their arrival, that another five Inchinnan girls had been engaged for work, leaving only three at the Depot. The evidence is that the Orphans Committee was diligent and paternalistic towards its charges, as were many others connected with them. For example one girl became pregnant by the son of her employer. The Committee cared for the girl and pursued the son and then his father for two years until receiving £50 in compensation. The surgeon on board the *Thomas Arbuthnot*, another orphan ship, felt compelled to continue his duties by accompanying 'his' girls into the hinterland to ensure that they had found suitable employers.

And may I add a short note on the *Inchinnan* to add a little more colour and background to the description of the girls' lives. She sailed on to New Zealand but on her return to Sydney had a part to play in another small aspect of Australian history that would have been the subject of all the talk in the girls' new homes. Gold had been found in California—a subject of conversation that they would never have heard back in Loughrea. There was a mad rush among Australian prospectors to get to California, and shippers and traders to make money out of them. Ships could not be chartered quickly enough and men clamoured to get on board so as not to miss out on new fortunes. The *Inchinnan* was the second ship to leave, carrying 219 men. And we thought 164 girls was a crowd. But these men would have willingly stood up all the way if it meant them being one of the first to get to the new goldfields. I wonder what the feelings of our three Lally girls were as they heard from the newspapers that their ship, the *Inchinnan*, was part of this exciting situation.

By this time all the *Inchinnan* girls had been found jobs. Mary Ann Lally, the eldest at about 16, was apprenticed to a Mr J. F. Heaney but wasn't with him a year before being dismissed on a charge of disobedience. Mr Heaney, a former convict, obviously didn't find his servant girl up to his exacting standards. She was found another position in March 1850. She married on 29 March 1853. This could have been at the end of a three year contract but it was unusual for a girl of that age to have such a long contract. Her husband, Isaac Walton, was an American who had come to Australia four years earlier as a merchant seaman but became a sawyer when he settled in Australia. They married at St Mary's Catholic Cathedral in Sydney and settled in the slum area of The Rocks. Their first recorded child was Edward who was born in March 1856. They moved out to Boughton's Creek and over the next 13 years had seven more children. Edward died at birth, and her third and fourth children died within a couple of weeks of each other at the ages of six and four. Life was hard in many ways. Throughout her life she stayed close to her sister, Margaret. Mary Ann and Isaac were witnesses at Margaret's marriage to Timothy O'Brien, a dairyman, in 1857. Margaret had eleven children. Their brother John Lally joined them from Loughrea in 1859. He married Bridget Clarke in 1868 and they had seven children. They all lived close to each other so one hopes their later lives were better than their childhood. Mary Anne lived to be 80, dying in 1914, but Margaret died at 55 in 1890 and John, at 45, in 1884. Nothing is known at the moment of Mary Lally. These were among the founding mothers and fathers of Australia, shipped there, not necessarily against their will, but because of the force of circumstances. Their lives were incredibly hard, not only in Ireland but in forging a living out of the virgin land of a new nation.

277 LIST of Immigrants per Ship "Inchinnan"

No.	Name		Married M.	Married F.	Single 14 years and upwards M.	Single 14 years and upwards F.	7 and under 14 years M.	7 and under 14 years F.	4 and under 7 years M.	4 and under 7 years F.	1 and under 4 years M.	1 and under 4 years F.	Under 1 year M.	Under 1 year F.
84	Kelly	Bridget				20								
85		Mary				22								
86	Kelly	Mary				15								
87	Kelly	Bridget				16								
88	Kelly	Catherine				17								
89	Kennedy	Biddy				17								
90	Kerrigan	Bridget				15								
91	Kerrigan	Betsy				15								
92	Killey	Margaret				28								
93	Lally	Margaret				14								
94		Mary Ann				16								
95	Lally	Mary				15								
96	Lennon	Lally				16								
97	Lyons	Mary				15								
98	McBride	Margaret				17								
99		Ann				14								
100	McCarrick	Margaret				19								
101	McCormick	Betty				18								
102	McCrae	Mary				17								
103		Letty				15								
104	McDermott	Mary				16								
105		Sarah				14								
106	McDermot	Ann				15								
107	McGarry	Honora				16								
108	McGowan	Mary				16								
109		Jane				16								
110	McGrath	Biddy				16								
111	McGuinness	Mary				18								

Arrived on the 13th February 1849

CALLING	NATIVE PLACE AND COUNTY	RELIGION	READ OR WRITE	REMARKS
Housekeeper	Lochreagh C. Galway	R Catholic	Neither	
Housemaid	do	do	Read	
Nurse Maid	Ballynass C. Mayo	do	Neither	
House Servant	Ballinasloe Galway	do	do	
do	Topnaconnel Roscommon	do	do	
do	Lochreagh C. Galway	do	Both	
do	C. Leitrim	do	Neither	
do	Clornteord C. Leitrim	do	Both	
Housemaid	Galway C. Galway	do	Read	
Housekeeper	Lochreagh do	do	do	
do	do	do	Both	
do	Ballymaguard, Galway	do	Read	
do	Buelick C. Donegal	do	Neither	
Nurse Maid	Lochreagh C. Galway	do	Read	
Housekeeper	Ballyshannon C. Donegal	do	Neither	
do	do	do	Both	
do	Eskey Sligo	do	Neither	
do	C. Galway	do	do	
Housemaid	C. Fermanagh	Protestant	do	
Housekeeper	C. Donegal	do	Read	
do	Bleak C. Donegal	R Catholic	Both	
do	Ballyshannon do	do	Neither	
do	Ballynass C. Mayo	do	do	
Housemaid	Ballinloe C. Sligo	do	do	
Housekeeper	Kilkoat C. Leitrim	do	do	
do	do	do	Both	
do	Tuam C. Galway	do	Neither	
do	Mohill Kings C.	do	do	

Part of the log recording the arrival of our girls in Sydney.
(New South Wales Government Archives)

11. A New World, 1848

We've followed the life of Patrick Lally for thirty years from his birth in 1818. The 1821 census and that dreadful newspaper report gave us a unique glimpse of his life in 1821. From then until the recorded birth of his son in London in 1848 he is lost to us in the mass of Irish peasantry, but we've assumed he grew to read and write and become a gardener in one of the big houses or nurseries in the Loughrea area. The other Patrick and his wife Mary left Loughrea for the USA before the Great Famine started. Many details survive of the journey of Mary Ann, Margaret and Mary Lally from Loughrea and Ballinasloe workhouses to Australia. It is perhaps most easy to feel sorry for these three young girls but, of all this group that we've called cousins, they seem to come out of the tragedy of Ireland better than the others. They were picked up by the authorities and treated with care. Now that all these members of the Lally family have left their beloved homeland to settle, each in their own new world, let us pull the threads of these three different stories together.

Patrick had settled well in London and had a good job. He had Elizabeth, who he'd marry when he could, and a new baby son, James, just three months old, and they would have changed his life and his attitude. The conditions of Ireland were frequently in the newspapers and he may have been in contact with his family in Loughrea. Perhaps his mother had died twelve years previously, but his father was probably still alive. In November 1848, when Patrick was thirty and established in his new life and when the three girls sailed for Australia, things were still at their worst in Ireland.

The population of Loughrea Workhouse was still climbing and would reach its peak, of 2,876 inmates, in February 1849. The 1851 census provides a good picture of what had happened in the famine years of the 1840s. The population of the country electoral districts immediately surrounding Loughrea fell by an enormous 39 per cent in just ten years: from 23,325 to 14,294. The population of Loughrea town had only fallen by 2 per cent: from 7,560 to 7,430. But the reason for this was that over 2,000, more than a quarter of the 1851 inhabitants, were in the workhouse and many had moved there from the surrounding area. Overall, the drop in population was 30 per cent and this was typical of the whole of the east of Co. Galway. Remember, too, that it was widely held that the 1841 census underestimated the true population. The censuses also listed the number of houses, both occupied and unoccupied. These fell by 33 per cent: from 5,198 to 3,475. The incredible conclusion, among so many incredible facts, is that, not only did over 9,000 people disappear from this small area in those ten years but so did over 1,700 houses. What sort of houses can go, in just ten years, from being classed as occupied or unoccupied to disappearing off the face of the earth?

Part of the answer is given by the *Illustrated London News* that reported that 71,130 holdings and houses had been 'done away with' in Ireland in 1849 alone, although it didn't explain from where it obtained this exact figure. These evictions would have been in the cause of larger holdings and more efficient farming but would certainly have meant the loss of home and livelihood and the destitution of over a quarter of a million people: in 1849 alone. Visitors to Connaught in the 1850s reported on the deserted countryside. They didn't encounter people on the road any more, the cabins that had been scattered across the hillsides were gone and where were all the children?

Another report in the *Illustrated London News* of January 1850 on the situation in County Clare, adjoining Galway to the south, stated that 43 percent of the population was dependant on poor law handouts. The other side of this coin was that

Poverty and dereliction in Ireland in 1850.

Poverty and dereliction in Ireland in 1850.

the rate levied on those with any income had risen to up to 18s 1¼d (91p) in the pound in order to support this. What, then, was the purpose of earning money and who could invest in the future with the remainder? Who would set up business there? The population, the report said, was now only one person per 2.75 acres so there was plenty of land to cultivate in order to feed everybody but what was the point? Those landlords that remained would not invest in crops and the workers were idle in the workhouses. The economy and life in general had completely collapsed. I think the modern description for Ireland at that time would be a 'failed state'.

Now we know the background of our family in Ireland it is clear why they had to leave and these descriptions of life there after they left show that they were lucky to have got out. They all seem to have had food on their tables in their new lives. Patrick, as he passed his thirtieth birthday in London was full of optimism in his new environment; the rapidly expanding capital of the world's greatest empire with opportunities all around. He and Elizabeth married in her Catholic Chapel in Isleworth, west of London, in 1851 and they would have nine children. But his hopes and plans were to come to nought and he was to end his life in Kensington Workhouse. What would he have made of the lives of his descendants, four and five generations on: their smart houses with central heating, fashionable clothes, luxurious and exotic food, entertainment, motor cars, and foreign holidays. Beyond his wildest imaginings!

Cecil Woodham-Smith, in his classic text book, 'The Great Hunger' summed up Patrick's later life and that of many others like him:

Very few of the Irish poor who fled from Ireland in the famine emigration were destined to achieve prosperity and success themselves; the condition to which the people had been reduced not only by the famine but by the centuries which preceded it was too severe a handicap and it was the fate of the Irish emigrants to be regarded with aversion and contempt. It was not until the second or third generation that Irish intelligence, quickness of apprehension and wit asserted themselves and the children and grandchildren of the poor famine emigrants became successful and powerful in the countries of their adoption.

Bibliography

1. The Course of Irish History, T W Moody & F X Martin, Mercier Press, 1994 revised and enlarged edition. One of the definitive textbooks on the whole span of Irish history

2. The Great Hunger (Ireland 1845-9), Cecil Woodham Smith, Hamish Hamilton, 1962
A definitive textbook on the subject.

3. Letters from Ireland during the Famine of 1847, Alexander Somerville (Ed. K D M Snell), Irish Academic Press, 1994. Letters published in The Manchester Examiner with detail and explanation of the situations he encountered in his travels.

4. The Irish Sketchbook of 1842, William Makepiece Thackeray, Nonsuch, 2005. Travel diary makes interesting background reading.

5. The District of Loughrea: Vol.1 History 1791-1918, Eds. Forde, Cassidy, Manzor, Ryan, Loughrea History Project, 2003. 34 essays on Loughrea history, several with very useful information on our period.

6. Print Culture in Loughrea, 1850-1900 (Reading, writing and printing in an Irish provincial town), Bernadette Lally, Four Courts Press, 2008. An MA thesis with a lot of interesting information and snippets from our period before 1850.

7. History of the O'Mullally and Lally Clan, D P O'Mullally, 1946, reprinted privately in 2001 by Mullinahone Press, California. A diatribe tracing the Lally clan back to the ancient Phoenicians in obscure detail.

8. The Workhouses of Ireland (the fate of Ireland's poor), John O'Connor, Anvil Books, 1995. Much good detail on the Poor Law and workhouses during the famine.

9. Barefoot and Pregnant? (Irish Famine Orphans in Australia), Trevor McClaughlin, 1991, The Genealogical Society of Victoria. Information on orphan girls scheme and great detail on the case of the 'Earl Grey'.

10. The Long Farewell, Don Charlwood, Penguin, 1981. Descriptions of the voyages of settlers under sail in the great migrations to Australia.

11. Australians and the Gold Rush (California and down Under, 1849-1854), Jay Monaghan. Sailing of the Inchinnan to Barbary Coast, then life of gold prospectors.

12. Tracing your Galway Ancestors, Peadar O'Dowd, Flyleaf Press, 2010. Detailed lists and explanations of finding your way through scant surviving records.

13. Irish Passenger Steamship Services, Vol.2, South of Ireland. D B McNeill. Publ. David & Charles, 1971

14. Kiltullagh Killimordally as the Centuries Passed, edited by Kieran Jordan. Published by Kiltullagh / Killimordally Historical Society, 2000. Extensive and detailed history of this small area of Co. Galway.

Acknowledgements

No matter what your interest there is somebody on the internet who shares it with you and so many of them have taken a great interest in my research into my family in Ireland. Much of my thanks must go to people I have met in this way: people who have enriched my story with detail. It is detail that I have sought in order to build an interesting story on the bare bones of birth, marriage, death, and census data.

Firstly I thank Michelle Mitchell who, in answer to my simple question on the website of 'Ireland Reaching Out' (Irelandxo.ie) took the trouble to send me the details of my family in a fragment of the 1821 census, thus taking my family history back a further 80 years and providing more information than I'd previously found elsewhere. Kieran Jordan helped me with so much information on the townland of Knockatogher and parish of Kiltullagh from where my family came. He even took me on a guided tour. Many others went beyond the call of duty, in my opinion, in answering my questions—from me, a complete stranger. Patria McWalter of Galway Archives helped with the Loughrea Board of Guardians Minute Books. Conor Nolan of the Irish Heritage Boat Association provided me with information about canals. Dawn Whitehead, a volunteer at the York Railway Museum 'Search Engine', took a great interest in the train our Lally girls travelled on. Christina Cassidy, Bernadette Lally and Judy and Geraldine at the Woodford Family History Centre have all produced useful information. I have not included all those recipients of one of my emails who have probably searched their archive on my behalf in vain, but spent their valuable time doing so. I thank them too.

My thanks go to Sandra Holmes who is descended from Mary Ann Lally who sailed to Australia on the *Inchinnan*, and Rita Gallagher whose forebears include Patrick and Mary Lally who emigrated to Pennsylvania. Both have provided much information on their ancestors' stories.

The final names are Kieran Jordan, again, of Kiltullagh and Stuart McKay the author of books on Tiger Moths who studied my manuscript and covered it with the very useful red ink of improvement.

Un-named helpers include those who have set up so many useful websites such as The National University of Ireland, Maynooth, National Centre for Geocomputation which has made available its analysis of census data and the University College, Cork Multitext Project in Irish History. There are dozens of websites providing information on aspects of this book; just two more worth a mention are galwaylibrary.ie/history/chapter14 and workhouses.org.uk which have much useful information on workhouses. I have also used several commercial sites such as ancestry, rootsweb, genes reunited.

Most of the illustrations are from contemporary newspapers such as the *Illustrated London News*. My thanks go to those such as Steve Taylor of Vassar College, NY, and Maggie Land Blanck who have made these available to me in high definition. Others have been sourced from The Mary Evans Picture Library.

My thanks go to my wife has put up with me shut in my office for over a year or out visiting archive centres while I pulled all my information into a book that I hope is interesting and worthwhile.

There are many more who I'm sorry not to have included. I hope that all my many helpers think the result is worth their patience with my interminable questions.

About the Author

Stephen Lally lives near London, England, and has had a successful career in sales and marketing. He has had a life-long interest in practical history. He is an acknowledged motoring historian and is actively involved with vintage cars. Among his other interests is working with young people.

Stephen has, over the years, built up a large collection of information, photographs, and memorabilia relating to his family history. His interest is in how people lived in previous times. He is not satisfied with the bare bones of a family tree that can be assembled from birth, marriage, death, and census information. The lives of previous generations were so different to ours, and he is keen to visualize this in the small details of their lives. To achieve this has involved widening the search for information beyond the normal genealogical sources.

Stephen now has more time to discover how his forebears lived nearly 200 years ago, and the breadth of this study, described in this book, is an eye-opener to all family historians, particularly those with ancestors from Ireland.